Lord, Teach us to Pray

by
Nicholas Hutchinson FSC

Illustrated by Steve Erspamer SM

Matthew James Publishing Ltd
Chelmsford, Essex

By the same author and publisher:

Praying Each Day of the Year

Vol.1 (January to April)   ISBN 1-898366-30-6
Vol.2 (May to August)   ISBN 1-898366-31-4
Vol.3 (September to December)   ISBN 1-898366-32-2

Walk in My Presence
ISBN 1-898366-60-8

First Published 1999 by:
Matthew James Publishing Ltd
19 Wellington Close
Chelmsford, Essex CM1 2EE

ISBN: 1 898366 65 9

Printed by J W Arrowsmith Ltd, Bristol

Dedicated to Pat,
severely ill with M.E.,
who calls to mind God's presence
and prays for people she will never meet

CONTENTS

FOREWORD

A warm welcome to this 50-day course of guided personal prayer! Some who use this book will recently have started or taken up again their journey of faith. Many will have been praying for years and are looking to further renew and refreshen their own prayer. Some will be using the book as a means of inviting others to explore various ways of praying.

In Luke's Gospel we read of the disciples saying to Jesus: *"Lord, teach us to pray, just as John taught his disciples"*. These words are not found early in the Gospel (where we might expect them to be recorded) but halfway through (Lk 11[1]). Are we to understand that the disciples did not pray prior to that time? Of course not, but we are reminded that praying is a process which needs to be renewed and revitalised from time to time, as is the case with the compelling invitation of Jesus to 'repent' (i.e. 'to turn around and realign ourselves in God's direction'). Indeed, 'praying' and 'repenting' go hand in hand. Neither can be 'static': each is very much an on-going process that repeatedly calls for renewed vision and commitment. That, after all, is how we progress in our human relationships. Refreshing and developing our prayer also helps us to remove some of the 'obstacles' that 'restrict' and 'impede' the Spirit, who has made his home in us and wants to pray in us (Rom 8[9,26]): the Spirit who works most fully when he can move as freely as the wind (cf Jn 3[8]).

We know and accept the reality that we are not yet perfect in love, yet sometimes tend to think that there is something terribly wrong in not being 'perfect' – right now – in faith and in prayer. If we can learn to be gentle with others, perhaps we need to grow to be more gentle with ourselves in this regard, knowing that *"we are all mercifully enfolded in the gentleness of God"*, as Julian of Norwich remarks. This book serves to remind us of the gentleness of God whose presence was not found in the violent storm, the earthquake or the fire, but in the gentle whispering breeze (1 Kings 19[9-14]).

For many people, the greater part of their time in prayer is spent in simply focussing on being in the presence of God, from which flows the rest of our prayer (and our lives). This book will have fulfilled its purpose if it helps readers to grow in awareness of being in God's presence.

May the Lord teach us to pray...

INTRODUCTION

"Prayer reaches our lives
as we begin to do things
we could not have done
unless we had prayed.
We begin to believe,
we seek forgiveness,
we love those
who would otherwise have been unlovable to us,
we attend to the important things in life.
Prayer is not a pious addition
to things we would have done anyway.
It is a force allowing things to happen
which could not have occurred without it."

Anthony Padovano

So what is prayer? St Teresa of Avila (1515-1582) writes that:

"Prayer is nothing else
than a close sharing between friends.
It means taking time frequently
to be alone with him
who we know loves us.
We let our masks fall,
and turn our hearts back to the Lord
who loves us,
so as to hand ourselves over to him as an offering
to be purified and transformed."

St John Baptist De La Salle mentions *"frequently being in the company of Jesus"*. This personal encounter, renewed each day, has a profound influence on our values, attitude and actions, because *"in his presence we can only love"* (as Evelyn Underhill records), affecting the way we see other people, and the way we think, work and relate. Growing in awareness of God's presence leads us to discover that the humdrum everyday world in which we *'live, move and have our being'* (Acts 17²⁸) is *'holy ground'* (Exodus 3⁵ – see 'Day 5').

This book shares resources and helps enable, exploring some of the many approaches that there are in praying. *"Prayer takes place in the heart rather than in the head"* (Carlo Carretto) and *"it is better in prayer to have a heart without words than words without a heart"* (Mahatma Gandhi). And so the words that are offered in this book are only a means to the end of being alone in God's presence: *"alone with him who we know loves us."*

Prayer is not about 'comfort' or about 'feeling good'. It is not an attempt to 'escape' from anything but is rooted firmly in daily life. Mother Teresa insisted that the chapel in her communities be on the street-side of the house, to remind the Sisters at prayer of the real world in which they live. For myself, in my own place of prayer in which I tend to look at the San Damiano Crucifix of St Francis (see 'Day 30') I keep in view a picture that reflects the ordinariness or the harshness of life. Presently I have a moving newspaper photograph that reflects the 1999 crisis in Kosovo, showing an ethnic Albanian lad, maybe aged 12. He is overwhelmed and cries as he walks away from the bloody corpses of his relatives, carrying his only possessions in a small plastic bag. Prayer brings us more in focus with the real world, and we remind ourselves in intercessory prayer that God's love enfolds everyone.

It is for each person to discover whichever ways of praying are the most appropriate during various stages and experiences of their faith-journey. From the late 1960s onwards, I have owed much to the inspiration expressed in the prayers of William Barclay, Michel Quoist, Michael Hollings and Etta Gullick, Huub Oosterhuis, Karl Rahner, Rex Chapman, Carmen Bernos de Gasztold, Frank Topping, Lucien Deiss, Mark Link, Peter de Rosa, David Adam, Donal Neary, Wendy Beckett and Denis Blackledge – and even Giovanni Guareschi for his down-to-earth prayers in the books of Don Camillo! I have also been strongly influenced in prayer (and in many other ways) through those whose lives I have shared – such as students and their families and teachers in schools where I have taught; individuals who are seriously ill; and many De La Salle Brothers who *"touch the face of God"* in their lives each day. These and others have shared with me the warmth of God's presence, the wealth of his love, and a lived experience of trusting in his providence.

HOW BEST TO USE THE MATERIAL FOR EACH DAY

1   In the context of other personal commitments of family life and work, etc, a choice needs to be made of an approximate time (and place) most appropriate for prayer. It would be important to set aside, say, 20 to 30 minutes of 'quality time', bearing in mind that someone who intends committing self to a loved one, but sets aside only the most 'worthless' period of the day, discovers that relationships are not likely to develop and progress! If at all possible, a time and place for prayer should be chosen such that there is little likelihood of being disturbed. Some who live alone disconnect the phone!

2   As time goes on, individuals discover that certain postures in prayer are the best for them. Keeping the spine vertical has always been thought to be helpful, whether sitting (on an easy or hard-backed chair, or possibly cross-legged whilst leaning against a wall or bed), kneeling or standing. Gestures in prayer can be very significant, as explored in the book.

3   It is essential to **have ready in advance whatever may be needed during the prayer**, otherwise the thread of prayer is broken and the resource becomes a distraction. If something is needed, it is listed at the start of each day's material. Occasional mention is made of the use of a candle, and scented candles in glass holders are now available in most supermarkets. If choosing to use a CD/cassette, it is necessary before starting to pray to **locate the start of the particular song**, so that it is ready to play when needed.

   If making use of the Internet for the time of prayer itself (rather than later in the day) the relevant page should be downloaded before starting to pray. **The optional use of the Internet is to help facilitate the prayer, not distract from it**. All preparations, then, must be made in advance.

4   It will be helpful to follow the 'structure' for the day, rather than starting part way through:
    - preparing what is needed from the list provided
    - relaxing
    - asking for the inspiration of the Holy Spirit
    - calling to mind God's presence
    - reflecting and praying
    - following up with 'action' of various kinds later in the day.

5   The key aim in prayer is *'to be in God's presence, to be in his company, to have a close sharing between friends'*. If little beyond the day's *'calling to mind God's presence'* is reached, all well and good! Some who have used draft copies of this book have sometimes returned later in the day to 'continue' to pray from the rest of the page (but always starting with *'relaxing'* and *'asking the Holy Spirit to lead in prayer'* and *'calling to mind God's presence'*). It is not necessary, though, to 'need' to finish a Day's material: the aim is to pray rather than necessarily to complete a task!

6   It is most important that there be pauses for silence. As the habit of prayer grows, silence will become more frequent, offering greater opportunity for God to 'slip in' (see 'Day 20'), to 'speak' in various ways at that and other times of the day. *'When I pray, co-incidences happen. When I don't, **they** don't"*, wrote William Temple. Again, it is preferable not to be determined necessarily to 'finish' what is printed for each day, if that is at the expense of remaining 'silent with God'.

7   When reading the written prayers in the text, it can make quite a difference to speak them slowly in a whisper rather than simply reading them silently. Sometimes it may also be helpful to read them more than once.

8   What is named as *'Action'* at the end of each Day's material is intended as "follow-up" in the next 24 hours. The process is also a means of promoting awareness of God's presence throughout the day.

9   It may be of benefit for the future to note what was of particular help: what 'went well'. This can be recorded simply by drawing a vertical line in the margin in pencil (rather than pen) beside the appropriate text. Pencil notes can also be made on the page (space has been provided to do so), or in a personal notebook, or typed on a word-processor. It would be best to do that after the day's prayer, rather than during it.

10 Some people keep a Prayer Journal, which may be handwritten or typed into a computer. What is recorded may be addressed to God, or (in the style of a diary) to self – or can alternate, as appropriate. Writing to God is, of course, a way of praying. Journalling can register something of the developing relationship with God, as comments and thoughts are recorded about the individual's 'journey' with God, especially after a period of prayer. Writing (and subsequently re-writing) such prayers led the author of this book to share prayers that others might wish to use.

The keeping of a Prayer Journal can help to focus one's thoughts and feelings. It can be encouraging to return and read something from the past that was written in similar circumstances to the present. It can be very touching at a later date to read about and be able to detect (perhaps in hindsight) how God was at work in one's life. Journalling can also help in the process of discerning what God may now be wanting of the individual.

A Journal might include biblical passages, others' prayers, and quotes from books or poems that are particularly meaningful and helpful. Two web-sites are listed at the start of the 'Internet' section of the 'Further Resources' at the back of the book.

In order to encourage the reader to 'identify' with the ways of praying in this book, the text is written in the first (rather than in the more usual second) person singular: "I" rather than "you", seeking to promote full involvement and "ownership" of the guided, personal prayer. This 'first person format' helps the text to be user-friendly, as well as providing consistency with the wording of the printed prayers.

Additional to the '50 Days' of the main part of the book are eight prayers written around some of the inspiring words of the hymn, 'St Patrick's Breastplate', which reflects on God's presence. As 'Lord, Teach us to Pray' emphasises the importance and centrality of focussing on the presence of God, so these additional prayers have been placed in the centre of the book, between Days 19 and 20.

The book is complete and entire without needing to play the hymns or use the Internet. Both are added bonuses to the text.

OPTIONAL USE OF SONGS/HYMNS

Some people like to listen to or sing along with a song/hymn as part of their prayer, and so a relevant hymn is named for most of the '50 days' in this book for those who might wish to make use of that resource. For convenience, hymns from three CDs/cassettes (sung by Marilla Ness) have been chosen:
- 'Come Back to Me'   (hymns chosen for 10 of the 'Days')
- 'He Touched Me'   (16 'Days')
- 'Holy One of Israel'   (16 'Days')

These can be bought at (or ordered for postal delivery through) most religious bookshops. There is an accompanying songbook which includes the words and music of all the hymns chosen in 'Lord, Teach us to Pray': 'The Marilla Ness Songbook' is listed under 'Further Resources' at the back of this book.

OPTIONAL USE OF THE INTERNET

Some may choose to make use of the named web-sites on the Internet but, to be clear, their use is to help facilitate prayer – and not to distract from it. Throughout the 50 days' course, details are given of more than 160 excellent web-sites or specific web-pages, with another 90 detailed in the 'Further Resources' section at the back of the book. Included are some religious paintings, and Sister Wendy Beckett remarks that "looking at art is one way of listening to God".

All the web-sites indicated in this book are listed (and updated) on the publisher's site: *www.matthew-james.co.uk*. Taking the details from there will save much time!

If there is no success in accessing a particularly long address, it may be possible to do so by breaking down the electronic address and first opening the main site e.g. for
http://gallery.euroweb.hu/art/d/duccio/buoninse/6maesta.jpg
it may be discovered on some occasions that it is easier first to access
http://gallery.euroweb.hu/
and then follow options to reach the named page.
If a 'server' is busy, it is possible that a web site or page may not be accessible at that particular time, but it may well be reached with no problems the following day. If still unable to access the site, it may be

advisable to enter its name (e.g. *'WebMuseum Paris'*) into a Search Engine such as *'Dogpile'*, which most effectively makes use of several search engines: *http://www.dogpile.com/*
That search may show a change of electronic address. It should be remembered that, in the nature of the Internet, some sites change address because of a change of Server.

Updates of all addresses will be kept on the publisher's site
http://www.matthew-james.co.uk
but, if not already listed there, the author would appreciate notification of any changes:
Nicholas@dls-liverpool.demon.co.uk

Use of the Internet can attune us to the inter-connectedness of life, and to the need to develop a growing sense of responsiblity for all manner of things. Contemporary technology can challenge us to question whether we look to a separation of the sacred and the secular (a dualism) or see their intermingling in daily life.

A CONCLUSION

As we walk each day beside other pilgrims along the hallowed road to Emmaus, let us remain faithful in prayer, so that our eyes may more readily be opened to recognise the risen Lord who chooses to accompany each of us on our journey, explaining the Scriptures and giving himself in the breaking of bread (cf. Lk 24).

Lord Jesus,
may we see you more clearly,
love you more dearly,
and follow you more nearly,
day by day.
"Lord, teach us to pray…"

(St Richard of Chichester)

(Lk 11¹)

Brother Nicholas Hutchinson, FSC
De La Salle House,
83 Carr Lane East,
Liverpool L11 4SF
Nicholas@dls-liverpool.demon.co.uk

Day 1   "I HAVE CALLED YOU BY YOUR NAME"   (Isaiah 43¹)

NEEDED

- *I could make use of a medley of two hymns on the CD/cassette, 'Come Back to Me' by Marilla Ness: 'When I feel the touch/Jesus, take me as I am'.*
- *If having access to the Internet, it would be especially helpful to download a particular icon, found at: http://www.clark.net/pub/webbge/jesmar35.jpg This inspiring icon is a very warm image of Jesus with his hand on the shoulder of a follower. It has been called 'The Icon of Friendship' and depicts the Coptic abbot Menas with Jesus, painted about 500A.D., and is found in the Monastery of St Catherine, Sinai. The icon appears on the cover of this book.*

RELAXING

Slowly I take two or three deep breaths and then, with eyes closed, I rest in peace and quiet as I breathe in my usual way again…

CALLING TO MIND GOD'S PRESENCE

I ask the Holy Spirit to inspire me and lead me in prayer…

I recall God's loving presence as I remind myself of his words, which I can repeat slowly several times:

> **"Do not be afraid, (MY NAME).**
> **I have called you by your name,**
> **and I am holding you by your hand."** *(Is 43¹, 41¹³)*

If I don't have the icon before me, I can still think of Jesus standing in front of me or beside me, with his hand on my shoulder. He has a clear expression of care and concern in his eyes, and has love in his heart.

(pause)

REFLECTING AND PRAYING

"Think of yourself for a moment.
There is no-one on this earth who is like you.
This may be just as well, but it is true.
You may have an identical twin
    who was removed at birth for all you know,
    but there is not, and cannot ever have been,
    nor will there ever be,
    a person who is exactly like you.
Even if it was possible to have
    exactly the same genes and chromosomes,
    the environment in which he (or she) grew up
    will have been different,
    and so will have become a different person.
It is not possible for someone else
    to have the same loves and hates, lusts and fears,
    anxieties, hopes and desires
    as you yourself have.
You are unique, you are yourself
    and there never has been – or can be –
    someone who is just like you,
    or who fills your place in the world.
And if religion is, as it claims to be,
    a personal relationship with God,
    your relationship with God
    will be something unique to yourself and him."

Gonville ffrench-Beytagh
'Encountering Light'

Father, perhaps you have best been described
    as "love"   *1 Jn 4⁸*
    and, as "love keeps no record of wrongs",   *1 Cor 13⁵*
    I rejoice in the completeness
    of your personal love and acceptance
    of each one of us.
Lead me each day to be faithful
    and grow closer to Jesus
    who calls me his friend.   *Jn 15¹⁴*
It is through him and in him, Father,
    that I am enabled to see you most fully: *Col 1¹⁵*
    you who call me by my name.   *Is 43¹*

The songs could be played.

God's loving me 100% is not because *I* am good, but because **he** is good. *"It is by grace that you have been saved – not by anything that **you** have done" (Eph 28).* God accepts me as I am. His love is not conditional on how someone might think I *'should'* be. Like the small tax-collector, Zacchaeus (*Lk 191-10*), who has to climb a tree to see Jesus, I am enabled to *'walk tall'*, affirmed as I am in the life-giving presence of Jesus.

God our Father,
    the qualities I see lived out so well
    in some people
    are a reflection of your own goodness,
    and I know
    that I have much to learn from other people
    who reflect your image and likeness   *Gen 126*
    in different ways.
Inspire me
    to respect others fully as my equals,
    seeing and loving in them
    what you see and love in them.

ACTION

I can set out to grow more aware of my true *'dignity'* – possibly looking at Michelangelo's inspiring fresco of God's creation of the (symbolic) first human being. God's finger is about to touch his beloved creation – it is a finger, and not a 'thumbs-down' directed to me. On *http://sunsite.auc.dk/cgfa/fineart.htm* access 'Michelangelo' and then 'The Creation of Man'.

A fine web-site offering a morning prayer and an evening prayer for each day of the week is: *http://www.cptryon.org/prayer/day.html*

Day 2   OFFERING MYSELF … A MORNING OFFERING

NEEDED

* *The song, 'Here I am, Lord', from the CD/cassette, 'He Touched Me'.*

RELAXING

Relaxing in a comfortable position, and with eyes closed, I take two or three slow deep breaths, and then I spend a couple of minutes simply monitoring my breathing, which may slow down and become more shallow.

CALLING TO MIND GOD'S PRESENCE

I put into words that I offer God my body and mind and spirit, that he may make good use of them in this time of prayer…

I ask Jesus to breathe into me his Holy Spirit, that he may inspire me in prayer…

I use some words of St Teresa to help focus on God's presence:

> **"Lord, you are closer to me**
> **than my own breathing,**
> **nearer than my hands and feet."**

REFLECTING AND PRAYING

There may be times when daily life appears to be tedious, monotonous or boring! I can pray:

> **Lord, inspire me to live in such a way**
> **that my choices each day**
> **and my commitment to live in a positive way**
> **may transform**
> **the negative into something positive,**
> **and the ordinariness of daily life**
> **into something extraordinary. Amen.**

John Wesley (1703-1791), the great preacher and founder of the Methodist Church, prayed these words:
> *"Lord, let me not live to be useless."*

Sadly, there are times when some people *mistakenly* think that they are *"useless"*. For some individuals, that sense of feeling *"useless"* or *"inadequate"* may arise from difficulties in childhood or relationships, in school or college, in work or unemployment, or with long-term health problems.

Many people, though, find that such an attitude begins to change for the better as they focus outwards in the service of others. Some individuals pray and offer their difficulties to God, as part of their total self-offering. The custom that many people have of praying a *'Morning Offering'* stems from this idea of the offering to God of *everything* about the individual: difficulties as well as the good things. Many find that, in the Lord's presence, those difficulties – or their *attitude* and *reaction* to those difficulties – are somehow *'transformed'*.

Some people – such as those amidst serious illness – may feel that they can take this *"offering"* a step further by linking *'service of others'* with *'prayer'*. They ask God to *"use"* their pain and frustration etc., to be of benefit and blessing for individuals whom they name in prayer, or for people they will never meet. Such outgoing generosity also helps to avoid destructive self-pity.

I raise both hands (and possibly my arms), as I pray:

Lord Jesus,
>   **I ask for the power of your Spirit**
>   **that I may remain positive**
>   **throughout all that happens**
>   **each day of my life,**
>   **knowing that nothing**
>   **can ever separate me**
>   **from your love.**   *Rom 8³⁹*
I know that your touch
>   **can change people and situations,**
>   **and so I ask you**
>   **to join me in offering to our Father**

not only the good things of this day,
but also any suffering and sacrifices
that I want to offer
cheerfully and lovingly,
and in a quiet and hidden way.
And so may any difficulties
and frustration and pain of this day
be transformed in your presence
for the benefit of other people.
Amen.

 The song, 'Here I am, Lord', could be played.

ACTION

I might consider adopting a practice that some people use in the first seconds of waking each morning. Even whilst still lying in bed I can simply trace a small cross with a finger or thumb on my forehead or heart – both are symbolic. That can be a gesture, a prayer, both of the offering of self, and of the desire to renew personal commitment to the crucified and risen Lord.

The gesture of making a very small cross on the forehead (or heart) can even be made whilst in public, without others noticing e.g. before a meal, before or on a journey, at the start of work.

"THE WORLD IS CHARGED WITH
Day 3   THE GRANDEUR OF GOD"

G M Hopkins

NEEDED

- *Something that reminds me of the beauty of God's creation e.g. a flower or plant, or a photograph or picture of the countryside. Or I could sit in a garden or park or beside water, or view other inspiring scenery.*
- *If inside, it would be helpful to have the hymn, 'Close to you/ I watch the sunrise' from the CD/cassette, 'Come Back to Me'.*

RELAXING

I pause to grow restful as I look at whatever is before me.

CALLING TO MIND GOD'S PRESENCE

I ask for the Holy Spirit to inspire me today as I pray:
> **Lord, send forth your Spirit**
> **to re-create me**
> **as you renew the face of our earth.**   *cf. Ps 104³⁰*

Slowly and thoughtfully I spend a few minutes repeating the words of this prayer several times:
> **Lord God, Creator of light,**
> **at the rising of your sun each morning**
> **let the greatest of all lights – your love –**
> **rise like the sun**
> **within my heart.**

The song, 'Close to you/I watch the sunrise', could be played.

REFLECTING AND PRAYING

I can talk to God about the ideas in these words:

> *"The beautiful is the spiritual*
> *making itself known*
> *through the senses"*   G. W. Hegel
>   *(1770-1831)*

As I reflect on the beauty ("the spiritual") in God's creation, I pray Psalm 104 from the Jewish Scriptures ('the Old Testament'), taking each line slowly and prayerfully:

Lord our God, how great you are,
    and I give thanks to you.
You stretch out the heavens like a tent,
    with the sun to mark our days of work
    and the moon for our nights of rest.

Your fingers created the earth
    and wrapped it with the ocean
    like a cloak.
There the ships sail,
    and beneath them
    glide the great sea creatures
    that you made to play with.
You pour down rain
    which the ground takes up.
You set springs gushing forth in the valleys,
    and streams that flow
    between the mountains,
    giving water to all that lives.

You make grass grow for the cattle
    and crops in abundance for our needs.
You bring goodness to the trees,
    and in their branches
    the birds build their nests.
Swarms of all living creatures
    are so many
    that they could never be counted.
What variety you have created, Lord,
    arranging everything so wisely!

You send your Spirit, and all things have life.
Fill us with your Spirit, Lord,
    and give us new life,
    and renew the earth that you love.

can add to the 'list' mentioned in the psalm, and can
say at the end of each new phrase:

**"The world is charged
with the grandeur of God."**

(G. M. Hopkins)

ACTION

can commit to memory the inspiring prayer, *"Lord
God, Creator of light"*, which is from the Armenian
Liturgy. It is the kind of brief prayer which, once
memorised, easily comes to mind as a means of
praying at odd moments from time to time –
particularly whenever the light of the sun is very
striking (however infrequently!).

We know that there were times when Jesus spent the
night in prayer (Lk 6¹²), and there were other occasions
when he started to pray *"long before daylight"* (Mk 1³⁵).
One of the greatest 'miracles of nature' is the renewal
of light with the breaking of the dawn, and it is likely to
be a prayerful experience if, in the coming weeks, I get
up at least once in sufficient time to witness the dawn,
slowly repeating the prayer, *'Lord God, Creator of light'*.
t is as dawn breaks on Easter Sunday that some
Anglican churches hold a service of the Resurrection.

An inspiring expression of the *'Canticle of Creation'* by
St Francis of Assisi, can be accessed on the Internet:
http://home.penn.com/franciscanstor/
Choose "forward", "Franciscan Poetry", and then
'Francis, the holy poet".

G.M.Hopkins; *"Thou mastering me God!"*:
http://www2.bc.edu/ ~ anderso/sr/hopkins.html

*The Nine Planets – A multi-media Tour of the Solar
System'* helps to stimulate the sense of wonder and
awe:
http://www.seds.org/billa/tnp/

"EYES TO SEE, PERCEPTIVENESS TO PERCEIVE"

(Anthony Bloom)

NEEDED

- *To be able to walk and sit in a garden or the countryside – either physically or in the imagination: possibly with the help of a scenic photograph or poster or picture from a magazine, or a flower, or a special piece of music.*

  Three web-sites that offer a wide range of inspiring photographs of natural scenes (e.g. landscapes, water, creatures, flowers) are:

  http://www.naturephotographs.com/
  http://www.yun.co.jp/~tomo/photo_e.html
  http://www.mountainzone.com/photo/gallery/intro.html

- *A medley of three hymns on the CD/cassette, 'Holy One of Israel': 'Open your eyes/See his glory/Reign in me'.*

RELAXING

I spend some moments relaxing amidst my surroundings...

CALLING TO MIND GOD'S PRESENCE

I ask the Holy Spirit to pray in me today...

(pause)

"The Holy Spirit is the invisible third party
  who stands between me and the other,
  making us mutually aware.
Supremely and primarily
  he opens my eyes to Christ.
But he also opens my eyes
  to the brother and sister in Christ...
  or the point of need,
  or the heartbreaking brutality
  and the equally heart-breaking beauty
  of the world.
He is the giver of that vision
  without which the people perish.   *Prov 29¹⁸*

We commonly speak about the Holy Spirit
  as the source of power.
But in fact he enables us
  not by making us supernaturally strong,
  but by opening our eyes."

John Taylor,
'The Go-Between God', pg 19

I pause to reflect on the presence of the Spirit....

REFLECTING AND PRAYING

The Russian Orthodox Archbishop Anthony Bloom once said that

"to meet God,
  one must have something in common with him,
  something that gives a person eyes to see,
  perceptiveness to perceive",

and in his poem, *'i thank You God for most this amazing day',* e. e. cummings talks of the awakening of the *'ears of my ears'* and the opening of the *'eyes of my eyes'.*

Lord Jesus,
  I ask you to open my eyes
  as you did with the blind man,   *Jn 9*
  so that I may really see.
Tune my ears
  as you did
  with the man who was deaf and dumb,   *Mk 7³¹⁻³⁷*
  so that I may really hear
  what you are saying to me.
May the many experiences of my senses
  remind me to be aware of others
  and of all that is around me.
May all that I experience
  lead me closer to you.

I could now take each of my senses in turn as a means of growing more aware/perceptive of what is around me, turning my thoughts and reflections into words of prayer e.g.

- **sight:** praying for the people and situations associated with a few of the things that I can see at the present moment.

- **hearing:** the sound of workmen laying cables in the road – praying about travel and communication.

- **touch:** being aware of different sensations through my fingertips; thinking of those who make much use of this sense. I pray, too, that God "touches" various named people and situations.

- **taste:** thinking of those who take their first taste for some time, such as someone dehydrated taking their first sip of water, a victim of famine about to eat some bread, a patient not able or allowed to eat or drink for some time, someone who hasn't for a long time tasted the salt of the sea air. I can pray about longing for something, and thirsting for God.

- **smell:** I could take experiences of various smells of the last 24 hours, and reflect and pray – food, flowers, aerosol sprays, fuel, the smell of clean places and clothes, unpleasant smells from factories, and smells of particular buildings such as a school or hospital or workplace.

♪ *Now or later I could play the medley of hymns: 'Open your eyes/See his glory/Reign in me'.*

ACTION

Later in the day I will think back to how I have been aware of others and situations during the day, and how I have detected God's world and his creativity through each sense.

Listed in 'Further Resources' are other books that have been found by many to be of great inspiration and of help in prayer.

e. e. cummings' poem may be found at:
http://members.xoom.com/dreamwine/cummings3.html

Day 5   TURNING ASIDE – LIKE MOSES – TO GOD'S PRESENCE

NEEDED

- *A pair of shoes/slippers placed beside a lit candle or a torch or lamp.*
- *A Bible for the Book of Exodus.*
- *It would be helpful to have the hymn, 'Holy Spirit, we welcome you' on the CD/cassette 'He Touched Me' by Marilla Ness.*

RELAXING

I spend two or three minutes letting silence and peace reach deep within me…

CALLING TO MIND GOD'S PRESENCE

*"If we really want to pray
we must first learn to listen,
for in the silence of the heart
God speaks."*   (T. S. Eliot, 1888-1965)

Another writer records that
*"Nothing in all creation
is so like God
as stillness…
I will sit and be silent
and listen to God's voice
within me."*   (Meister Eckhart, 1260-1327)

In silence I call to mind that God is present with me.

(pause)

I ask the Holy Spirit to inspire me today as I pray…

♪ *The hymn, 'Holy Spirit, we welcome you", could be played.*

REFLECTING AND PRAYING

I read Exodus 3[1-6], telling of Moses and the burning bush: his unexpected encounter with God. Moses takes off his shoes in the presence of God.

I pause for a few minutes to remind myself that, as with Moses, God is indeed with me now.

(pause)

It is true that we need to be able to "*see*". The poet Elizabeth Barrett Browning (1806-61) expresses this well as she reflects on the same Biblical passage of Moses and the burning bush:

> *"Earth is crammed with heaven,
> and every common bush
> is afire with God.
> But only he who sees
> takes off his shoes;
> the rest sit round
> and pluck blackberries."*

(pause)

**God our Father, Creator of light,
    lighten my darkness
    with the brilliance of your presence.
Lead me to discover you
    in all the people you place into my life
    and in the events and places
    that make up my life each day. Amen.**

ACTION

Later in the day I can read this poem (*'The Bright Field'*) of R. S. Thomas (b.1913) and I will pray to grow in awareness of God's presence in the ordinary events of life.

I have seen the sun break through
to illuminate a small field
for a while, and gone my way
and forgotten it. But that was the pearl
of great price, the one field that had   (cf. Mt 1345)
the treasure in it. I realize now
that I must give all that I have
to possess it. Life is not hurrying

on to a receding future, nor hankering after
an imagined past. It is the turning
aside like Moses to the miracle
of the lit bush, to a brightness
that seemed as transitory as your youth
once, but is the eternity that awaits you.

BRINGING OTHERS TO THE LORD
Day 6   IN PRAYER (Moses prays)

NEEDED

- *St John's Gospel (for the 'Action').*
- *It would be helpful to have the song, 'I lift my hands', from the CD/cassette, 'Holy One of Israel'.*

RELAXING

I spend a few moments with my eyes closed, taking in the peace that can come with relaxation.

CALLING TO MIND GOD'S PRESENCE

I ask the Holy Spirit to inspire and lead me in prayer today…

We read in the Jewish Scriptures ('the Old Testament') that *"God would speak with Moses as a person speaks to a friend"* (Ex 33[11]). In the Christian Testament ('the New Testament') Jesus says: *"I call you friends"* (Jn 15[14]).

St Ignatius Loyola (1491-1556) writes that *"we are to speak to God as a friend speaks to a friend"* (Spiritual Exercises, 54). In that manner I pray to him now:

> **Lord, you call me by my name**
> **and you call me your friend.**
> **I pause for a few moments**
> **to bring myself into your presence,**
> **friend to friend.**

(pause)

REFLECTING AND PRAYING

A joke has been told of a person with an injured hand who holds out both limbs and prays: *"Lord, make my hand like the other one"* – and the good hand worsens! We are reminded, of course, that there is no need in

prayer to spell out in great detail what we mean, or be very precise in our use of language. In prayer we don't need to ensure that verb endings agree, or avoid split-infinitives, or even state exactly why we are praying for a particular person! Nor is there any need to mention someone's address to God, as though he doesn't know who we are talking about, and might do something for the 'wrong' person instead!

Prayer reflects our relationship with God, *"friend to friend"*. Our prayer is whatever may be the most appropriate at the moment, and will probably be in various forms at different times: such as in words, in music, in silence, in the use of symbols (picture-images).

A picture-image in the Jewish Scriptures may help us to appreciate that God can work powerfully as we support one another in prayer. Moses prays for the people, that they may be delivered in battle. Symbolically he raises his arms in prayer.

> *"As long as Moses kept his arms raised,*
> *Israel had the advantage;*
> *when he let his arms fall,*
> *the advantage went to their enemies.*
> *But Moses' arms grew heavy…*
> *and Aaron and Hur supported his arms,*
> *one on either side."*

(Ex 17[8-12])

Without necessarily wanting to focus on "battle", we are presented with an appealing image of the 'effectiveness' of praying for others, especially when we support one another in prayer (as did Aaron and Hur). God can work powerfully!

 The song, 'I lift my hands', could be played.

Some elderly or housebound people associated with a school or hospital or hospice, state that they will pray for the people there at a certain time each day, often using a set prayer.

Alfred Lord Tennyson (1809-1892) wrote:

"More things are wrought by prayer
Than this world dreams of.
Wherefore, let thy voice
Rise like a fountain for me night and day."

It is of great benefit to others if we develop the habit (or custom) of naming people before the Lord. It also serves as a reminder to those who may be physically remote from other people, that none of us need feel cut off, or feel unable to do something that can benefit others.

I can raise my arms (or just my hands) in prayer in quietness and in privacy. Closing the eyes often helps, and I remind myself again that I am in God's presence. I *"raise up"* to the Lord several people, picturing them or naming them.

ACTION

In John's Gospel we read of two occasions when Andrew *brings someone to Jesus*. One way that I can bring people to Jesus is to bring them into his presence in prayer, as I *look outwards* in loving concern. I can read in **John 1**40-42 how Andrew says to his brother, Simon Peter: *"We have found the Messiah"*, and he *brings* Simon to Jesus. In **John 6**1-15 it is Andrew who *brings* to Jesus the small boy with five loaves and two fish, which Jesus will use to feed the five thousand. During the day, as I meet individuals, I can *"bring them"* to the Lord, naming them in his presence.

––––––––––––––––––––––––––

Prayer requests and intercessions are included in a fine site for personal prayer that is specific to days of the year:
http://www.missionstclare.com/
– Daily Prayer from the Anglican/Episcopal *'Book of Common Prayer'*. Icons are shown and hymns are played.

(See also Day 46)

Day 7   FATHER, YOU ARE THE POTTER, AND WE ARE THE CLAY

NEEDED

- *It would be useful to have a piece of pottery or an earthen plant pot or, preferably, something that is malleable e.g. clay, plasticine, or BluTack.*

RELAXING

I close my eyes whilst feeling the piece of pottery or something malleable, bearing in mind that some people with hypertension are encouraged to spend about 15 seconds squeezing something (even just a fist) and then compare that tension with the relaxation of muscles as the grip is let go.

CALLING TO MIND GOD'S PRESENCE

In the ordinariness of my life now, I pause for a few moments to bring to mind that I am in God's loving presence, as I say several times these words of Martin Luther (1483-1546):

"Rest in the Lord;
*   wait patiently for him.*
Be silent before God
*   and let him mould you.*
Keep still,
*   and he will mould you*
*   to the right shape."*

REFLECTING AND PRAYING

Lord God, you are our Father:
    you the potter, and we the clay.   *Is 64⁷*
Your own hands
    have shaped us and modelled us.   *Job 10⁸*
Re-form us now
    so that we may more closely resemble

the image and likeness
    of Jesus, your Son.
Lead us to live in such a way today
    that others may recognise
    that we are made by your hands.
Inspire us to realise
    and lead others to appreciate
    that each of us
    is your work of art.   *Eph 2*

I can use the symbolic action of raising a small saucer or plate, or I can cup and raise my hands a little as I use the following words of Martin Luther. It may be helpful to re-word them as a prayer, repeating them slowly several times:

"I have held many things in my hands,
*   and I have lost them all,*
*   but whatever I have placed in God's hands,*
*   that I still possess."*

In 1983 Father Pedro Arrupe, leader of the religious order of the Jesuits, reflected on his experiences following a severely disabling stroke:

"More than ever,
*   I now find myself in the hands of God.*
This is what I wanted all my life
*   from my youth.*
And this is still the one thing I want.
But now there is a difference:
*   the initiative is entirely with God.*
It is indeed a profound spiritual experience
*   to know and feel myself*
*   so totally in his hands."*

Comedian, singer and presenter of religious programmes, Sir Harry Secombe, suffered a stroke in 1999, leaving him paralysed on one side, although physiotherapy has been of great help. Attempting to

ome to terms with his disability, he puts himself into
he hands of God, and has said: *"God's got pretty safe
hands – he'd make a wonderful goalie!"*

can commit to memory and repeat several times these
words of a psalm, as I raise slightly my upturned hands:

"Lord, my life is in your hands." *Ps 31 16*

ACTION

A few times during the day I can raise my upturned
hands (raising them even only a few centimetres) and I
pray these words of a hymn:

Spirit of the living God,
melt me, mould me,
fill me, use me.

PRAYING FOR GOD'S BLESSING
Day 8   ON OTHERS

(Zechariah and his son, John the Baptist)

NEEDED

- *It would be helpful to have the song, 'Make us one, Lord' from the CD/cassette, 'The Holy One of Israel'.*

RELAXING

Knowing that it takes 60 muscles to frown and only 13 to smile, I spend at least 30 seconds smiling widely! Especially when practised alone early in the morning (even whilst washing) it can be surprising how this gesture can contribute to a positive outlook in the day ahead. It can also be a means of letting tension go, and relaxing.

CALLING TO MIND GOD'S PRESENCE

I ask the Holy Spirit to inspire me today as I pray…

Lord, you said that when two or three
   would gather together in your name,
   then you would be present with them.
I am praying by myself
   but I am uniting myself
   with many individual Christians
   throughout the world
   who, though separate,
   are gathered together in another sense
   to pray to you,
   and I trust that you are with me now.

(pause)

REFLECTING AND PRAYING

Many Christians in this country (and in every country throughout the world) use a book called *"The Prayer of the Church"* as they pray each day. Psalms and prayers and readings from throughout the Bible are used, along with prayers for the needs of our world.

Those who pray in that way can sense support and encouragement, realising that many others throughout the world (and in many different circumstances and languages) are using the same prayers. It can help in appreciating that we are 'inter-connected' as sons and daughters of God our Father, and are brothers and sisters of Jesus and of one another.

♪ *I could play the hymn, 'Make us one, Lord'.*

Used at Morning Prayer each day is a prayer expressed by Zechariah, as he addresses his baby son, John, who will be the one to *"prepare the way"* for Jesus. Zechariah prays this blessing on his son, John the Baptist – *"and you, little child…"* – telling John that God is calling him, and that God's promises will come to fulfilment through him. As I pray these words it may be helpful to focus on *one* individual whom I might picture before me, just as Zechariah prays for his son: *"You, my child"*.

Blessed be the Lord our God
   because he has come to his people
   and set us free.
He has raised up a powerful Saviour for us,
   born a descendant of David.
Through his prophets of old
   he promised to save us
   from the hands of those who hate us.
So he shows his loving kindness,
   as promised to our father Abraham.
Yes, he has freed us
   so that, without fear,
   we can worship him and serve him
   in his very presence
   all the days of our lives.
As for *you, little child,*
   you, too, will be called God's prophet,
   for you will go before him
   to prepare the way
   for his coming amongst us,
   as the prophets promised from of old.

will be for *you, my child,*
  to tell his people
  that he will save them and forgive them,
  and be gentle and merciful.
you, my child, must tell them
  that he will bring the rising sun to visit us,
  giving light to those who live in darkness
  and in the shadow of death,
  guiding our feet along the way of peace.

Lk 167-79

can pray God's blessing on individuals who are
entrusted to my care, on my family and friends, and on
those I will meet today, just as Zechariah prayed this
blessing on his own son, the infant John the Baptist…

(pause)

think now of some of God's blessings in my own life,
and I thank him.

ACTION

When I hear the siren of an emergency vehicle, I can
make it my practice to pray for God's blessing on all the
individuals concerned. Some people do likewise when
they hear the ring of the phone or the door bell.

The *'Prayer of the Church'* – the psalms and prayers and
readings used by many people across the world – are
arranged in a 4-week cycle. An introduction to this way
of praying would be to explore a shorter prayer service
on the same lines. *'Caritas: A Virtual House of Prayer'*
can be accessed at:
http://www.cptryon.org/caritas/index2.html

The full book for the 4-week cycle can be bought, but
each day's prayer can be accessed daily on the Internet
at:
http://www.universalis.com/cgi-bin/display/

NEEDED

- *It would be useful to have the CD/cassette, 'He Touched Me', with the medley of songs: 'Lift up your hands/I love you, Lord/He touched me'.*

RELAXING

I sit in a comfortable position and close my eyes. Slowly I move my shoulders up and down and roundabout and then move my head around in a circular way, helping to remove any tension that might be there.

Slowly I look at both sides of each hand in turn, noticing any scars and individual marks. I look at the details of my fingertips, reminding myself that no-one has ever had or will ever have the same fingerprints as my own. Ear-prints and foot-prints that are sometimes taken of babies in hospital also reflect our individuality, as does our own DNA, I am truly special, and I relax in that conviction. I give thanks for God's love for me as a unique individual…

CALLING TO MIND GOD'S PRESENCE

God our Father,
   your Son became a human being
   and lived among us:
   fully human
   as well as fully divine.
As I look at my hands
   and am aware of my own body,
   I pause to remind myself
   that your Son
   did indeed take on
   the very same flesh and existence
   as my own.
I call to mind
   that he is with me now,
   as he promised to be.

(pause)

I ask the Spirit to pray in me…

REFLECTING AND PRAYING

Some individuals set out to pray at around 12-00 midday each day, knowing that at that time they can be united with many others who are praying at that particular time. Some even set a wristwatch alarm for 12.00 to remind them to join others in prayer and, whether at work, at school, at home, or whilst shopping, others need not know that they are praying quietly.

At about 12.00 (and also at about 6.00pm) some Christians of the Catholic tradition pause to focus their prayer on God becoming a human being. As Mary said *"Yes"* to the invitation to be the mother of Jesus, I, too, can offer myself to be part of God's plan, using the prayer called *'The Angelus'*:

> **The angel of the Lord declared unto Mary,**
> **And she conceived by the Holy Spirit.**

> **Behold the handmaid of the Lord:**
> **Be it done to me according to your word.**

> **And the Word was made flesh**
> **And dwelt amongst us.**

(Lk 126-38, Jn 11⁴

♩ *The songs could be played.*

God our Father,
   may the birth in our midst
   of Jesus, your Son,
   call us to treasure
   what is most deeply human.
Touch our hearts
   that we may see your Word made flesh
   in those to whom you send us.

(inspired by a prayer
in the Roman Missal)

ACTION

A few times during the day I could pray the following words (which I might carry with me on a small piece of paper, helping to commit them to memory). On each occasion I pray the words slowly several times:

In the fullness of time, Lord, *Gal 44, Eph 1 10*
you were born amongst us,
and you live with us now.

When the time and circumstances are appropriate in the future, I could mention to someone that I will be remembering them in prayer at a specific time. In addition to whatever way the Lord himself will act, this can be a powerful means of expressing care and support as the individual realises at the named time, that someone is praying to the Lord for them.

I might look on the Internet at a site which focuses on world-wide prayer at 12-00 midday:
http://www.users.surfaid.org/ ~ monkton/index.htm

Millet's painting, 'The Angelus', showing peasants praying in a field, may be viewed on the Internet at:
http://home.connectnet.com/joe/millet/

One of several paintings of the Nativity by Georges de la Tour (displayed in Rennes) may be accessed at:
http://www.kimbellart.org/klatour.htm

A web-site that explores the place of Mary in the lives of Christians (and which makes use of art) is at:
http://www.cptryon.org/compassion/mary/index.html

NEEDED

- *The inspiring painting, 'The Baptism of Christ', by Piero della Francesca (painted about 1442), can readily be downloaded from the Internet at 'The WebMuseum, Paris':*
  http://www.southern.net/wm/paint/
- *The song, 'Do not be Afraid' from the CD/cassette, 'Come Back to Me' could be used in today's 'Action'*

RELAXING

Once in a comfortable position, I close my eyes and slowly take a few deep breaths, and then relax as my breathing becomes more usual.

CALLING TO MIND GOD'S PRESENCE

With breath/wind being a symbol of the Holy Spirit, I breathe out as far as I can, expelling the air from my lungs, and then slowly breathe in, thinking of the air filling my lungs to capacity, and the Holy Spirit filling my whole self.

With eyes closed I can pray:

Spirit of God,
come fill my life…

REFLECTING AND PRAYING

The author of *'Pilgrim's Progress'* – John Bunyan (1628-1688) – wrote about his earlier severe mental breakdown: *"I was more loathsome in mine own eyes than was a toad, and I thought I was so in God's eyes, too."* Bunyan (like many others) came to discover that none of us can *"earn"* God's love. Instead, God's love is freely given, and our love is a response: *"We are to love, then, because God loved us first"* (1 Jn 4[19]).

The GOOD NEWS of God's personal love is reflected not only in the actions and words of the father in the story of the lost/prodigal son (Lk 15[11-32]) but also in the words of God the Father towards Jesus: *"You are my much-loved Son".* We read of these words both at the Baptism and the Transfiguration of Jesus (Mk 1[11]; 9[8]).

John the Baptist was known as a prophet, and people queued at the River Jordan to be dipped and immersed by him in the water. It was a sign of wanting to be cleansed from sinfulness, re-directing their lives to God. Jesus himself, preparing for the start of his ministry, joined the queue of people, wanting to identify himself with them. Something extraordinary happened:

> *'As soon as Jesus came up out of the water, he saw the heavens open and the Spirit, like a dove, coming down upon him. And a voice came from heaven: "You are my Son, the Beloved; I am well pleased with you." '*

(Mk 1[9-11])

I spend a few moments with my eyes closed, picturing myself present as the next person in line to be baptised by John.

(pause)

God our Father, open my eyes
to discover the vision
that you have for me.
Lead me to grow in faith and confidence
that you have truly made me
in your own image and likeness,
and you call me by my name.
As with your Beloved Son, Jesus,
you say to me:
"You are my well-loved son/daughter,
and my favour rests on you."
Lead me, Father, to hear that message
in the many different ways
in which you convey it to me.

mpower me with your Spirit
   that I may grow
   as the person you call me to be.
nable me to bring the Good News
   to the people you place in my life,
   so that I may confirm for others
   that they, too,
   are your well-loved sons and daughters.

will remind myself several times during the day of the
eart of the Good News, that God calls me by name and
ays:
   "You, (NAME),
      are my much-loved son/daughter,
      and I am very fond of you."

The song, 'Do not be Afraid', could be played.

CTION

s I see particular people today I can also focus on *their*
being blessed, as I say silently:
   "You are God's son/daughter,
      and he loves you greatly."

----

he word 'baptise' comes from the Greek, meaning 'to
ip'.

The Baptism of Christ' by Joachim Patenier and the
painting of the same name by Andrea del Verrocchio
can be downloaded from the Web Gallery of Art at:
http://gallery.euroweb.hu/index.html

The Return of the Prodigal Son' by Rembrandt (painted
about 1662) can be accessed via:
http://www.southern.net/wm/paint/

*hotos of the River Jordan may be accessed at:
http://www.holy-land-online.com/jordan_river/gallery.htm

"POINTS OF DEPARTURE TO A DESERT, SILENCE, SOLITUDE"

Day 11

(Catherine de Hueck Doherty)

NEEDED

- *The Gospel of St Mark*
- *The song, 'Come back to me' from the CD/cassette of the same name.*

RELAXING

I close my eyes and think of places where I have been alone (not necessarily lonely). Was the solitude of help to me, maybe in relaxation or in finding a better balance in life, in gaining perspective, or in the joy of appreciation or wonder?

(pause)

Terry Waite, freed in 1991 from 1,763 days as a hostage in the Lebanon, writes of learning *"how to turn deep loneliness into creative solitude."*

CALLING TO MIND GOD'S PRESENCE

I ask the Holy Spirit to lead me as I pray today…

We read in the Gospel, Lord,
   that you went away to lonely places
   to pray.
In my busy days of noise and action,
   remind me of my need
   for time alone
   and for peace and quiet
   and silence within.
Be with me now
   as I pause for a few moments
   in quietness.

(pause)

REFLECTING AND PRAYING

Several times over I will read just two verses from St Mark's Gospel, Chapter 6, verses 30 and 31…

I pause to think over these two verses and then re-word them as a prayer.

(pause

The following passage explores the realisation that ever 'busy' places can become 'points of departure to solitude':

"Deserts, silence, solitudes are
   *not necessarily **places***
   *but **states of mind and heart**.*
These deserts can be found in the midst of the city,
   and in every day of our lives.
We need only look for them
   and realize our tremendous need for them.
They will be small solitudes,
   little deserts, tiny pools of silence,
   but the experience they will bring,
   if we are disposed to enter them,
   may be as exultant and as holy
   as all the deserts of the world,
   even the one God himself entered.
For it is God who makes solitude,
   deserts and silences holy.

"Consider the solitude
   of walking away from the train or bus
   to our home in the evening,
   when the streets are quieter
   and there are few passers-by.
Consider the solitude that greets you
   when you enter your room
   to change your office or working clothes
   to more comfortable, homely ones.
Consider the solitude of a housewife,
   alone in her kitchen,
   sitting down for a cup of coffee
   before beginning the work of the day.
Think of the solitudes afforded
   by such humble tasks
   as housecleaning, ironing, sewing.

"One of the first steps towards solitude
   is a departure.
Were you to depart to a real desert,
   you might take a plane, train or car to get there.

But we're blind to the 'little departures'
   that fill our days.
These 'little solitudes'
   are often right behind a door which we can open,
   or in a little corner
   where we can stop to look at a tree
   that somehow survived the snow and dust
   of a city street.
There is the solitude of a car
   in which we return from work,
   riding bumper to bumper on a crowded highway.
This too can be a 'point of departure'
   to a desert, silence, solitude."

(Catherine de Hueck Doherty:
'Poustinia: Christian Spirituality
of the East for Western Man')

♪ *The song 'Come back to me' could be played,*
   and I can focus in prayer on the words:
      "The wilderness will lead you
         to your heart where I will speak."

ACTION

Today I will spend at least two periods of time as *'points
of departure to a desert, silence, solitude...'*: opportunities
to be close to God amidst the busy-ness of daily life.

Mention of *'going away to a lonely place to pray'* can be
found in Mt 14¹³; Mk 1³⁵, 6³¹; Lk 4⁴², 9¹².

Evelyn Underhill re "lifting my eyes to the eternal hills",
and "wanting", "having", "doing" and "being":
ttp://www2.bc.edu/~anderso/sr/underhill.html

Some meditations and prayer services:
ttp://cptryon.org/prayer/season/index.html

Catherine de Hueck Doherty and Madonna House:
ttp://www.mv.igs.net/~madonnah/doherty/index.html

Today's prayer will simply focus on placing myself in God's presence.

NEEDED

A bowl of water and a towel.

RELAXING

With my eyes closed and my fingers touching the water, I think of good memories of some places I have visited that have been associated with water – the sea, rivers, lakes, ponds, snow.

(pause)

CALLING TO MIND GOD'S PRESENCE

I pray that the Holy Spirit will lead and guide me during this time of prayer, as I remind myself that I am

> *"a temple of God,*
> *with the Spirit of God living in me."*   1 Cor 3¹⁶

(pause)

In today's society, many people feel uncomfortable with silence, and will do anything to fill it! Yet it is in silence that we can discover ourselves and meet God. St Teresa of Avila (1515-1582) says:

"It is not with many words that God hears us, but in the silence of our longing."

I am setting out, Lord,
   to spend some moments of quietness
   amidst the noise and busy-ness of the day,
   making myself more aware
   of the noises around me
   – both within this room and beyond...

(pause)

The silence within me
   and the gentle noises around me
   remind me that as I close myself
   to all that makes me
   busy and pre-occupied,
   I can open myself
   to the quietness and gentleness
   of your loving presence with me.

REFLECTING AND PRAYING

Words of others can often be of help in prayer. I reflect and pray on these words of Cardinal Basil Hume (1923-1999):

"When adults play hide-and-seek with young children, the children can never lose. It would be a bad game if adults hid in some place where they could not be found. We make certain that we can be. If, by chance, the child still fails, then we go in search. Is there not something similar in God? He gives us any number of opportunities to find him. And even if we become distracted and stop looking, he will take an initiative – a happy experience possibly, or one involving tragedy or sadness – and come looking for us. He wants us. Never doubt that.

"It is only in the experience of praying that we become aware not only that we seek God, but that God is always seeking us. That realisation can come in all sorts of ways. Often we come closest to him when we experience weakness and suffering. God can speak to us when we are most desolate. Our search often begins when tragedy befalls. We then begin to look.

"We are slow to understand that God is searching for us, because we are deaf and blind. Our modern civilisation with its emphasis on scientific and technological achievement is in danger of making us less and less receptive to God, and so less inclined to listen and look. But when science and human skill fail us and we feel helpless and weak, that can be a golden moment. We are no longer self-sufficient."

('To be a Pilgrim', p 49-51)
(pause

Some of the psalms from the Jewish Scriptures make use of the imagery of water. I can commit to memory these words and repeat them several times as I touch some water:

> "To you, Lord,
>   I stretch out my hands.
>   Like a parched land
>   I am thirsty for you."   *Ps 143⁶*

ACTION

I will take 'time out' during the day ahead: at least a couple of short periods in which I will *"set myself in silence and peace"* in God's presence (Ps 130²).

Jn 41-42 tells of the encounter of Jesus with the Samaritan woman at the well. Jesus says to her: *"Whoever drinks the water that I shall give, will never be thirsty again."* A sculpture of this scene by Benedetto da Maiano (b. 1442) can be viewed at the *'Web Gallery of Art'* at:
http://gallery.euroweb.hu/art/b/benedett/samarian.jpg

'Wellsprings' is a web-site on prayer:
http://freespace.virgin.net/well.springs/

Day 13   THE PARALYSED MAN LET DOWN THROUGH THE ROOF

NEEDED

- *The Gospels*
- *The hymn, 'The Spirit of the Lord', from the CD/cassette 'Come Back to Me', or 'Lay your hands' from 'He Touched Me'.*

RELAXING

I close my eyes and focus first on relaxing the muscles in my shoulders, and then gradually in turn the muscles in my arms, hands, legs and feet.

CALLING TO MIND GOD'S PRESENCE

Trusting in your goodness
and great mercy, Lord, I come:
sick – I come to my Saviour;
hungry and thirsty – to the well of Life;
needy – to the King of Heaven.

(Thomas à Kempis, 1380-1471)

I pause to remember that he is with me...

I ask the Spirit to guide me in prayer today...

♪ *'The Spirit of the Lord'*

REFLECTING AND PRAYING

I read through the account of Jesus curing someone who was paralysed: *Mark 21-12*:

(I pause to read the Gospel passage)

I read through the same passage a second time, imagining myself present during the event: either as the person who was paralysed, or as one of the four who helped, or as the owner of the house, or as a neighbour, or as someone who is curious as to who Jesus is.

(I pause to read the passage a second time)

I can read and pray through the following meditation on this Gospel passage, using in prayer the idea of *"placing myself into the scriptures"*. The reflection only goes so far, encouraging me to continue it, to pray it as the scene enfolds before me.

My friend is ill. He's not getting better. I've heard that a person called Jesus from Nazareth is visiting Capernaum today (that's the village nearest to ours). People say that Jesus is holy, and that he can do things that only God can do. Four of us have decided to take our friend to see Jesus. I know that lots of people are likely to gather round him but, if we can't get close enough, at least we won't have done any harm, and our friend will know that we care enough about him to have tried.

We carry our friend on a stretcher, although it's really too hot today to be doing that, and dust is being kicked up as we walk along. We arrive in the village, and I can see some other friends of mine in the distance. A crowd is gathering, so it's pretty obvious where Jesus is.

The five of us chat amongst ourselves, and our friend who is ill is telling us not to go to all the trouble, but we are determined to do what we can for him. I'm persistent enough, so I've started to push my way through the crowd, but it's just impossible to get near the door, and people are telling us to be quiet because they want to hear what Jesus is saying.

We're next to some steps that lead up towards the flat roof of the low building, and someone nudges me to try going up there. It's tricky, and we don't want our friend to have further injury or become more ill as we carry him up.

Once we're above, we tie a fisherman's ropes to the handles of the stretcher. I hear a voice below; it must be Jesus. He says: *"I am the light of the world. Those who follow me will not be walking in the dark."* At that very moment, one of my friends starts to pull apart some of the branches that provide the shaded roof of the house he light streaming in catches the attention of someone it must be the owner of the house, because he's not ɔo pleased, from what he's saying! But Jesus holds him ack, and encourages us. With the ropes, we're able to ɘt the stretcher down slowly and gently – I wonder if ur paralysed friend thinks it's like being lowered into a rave? Yet Jesus is looking up and saying: *"I am the esurrection and the Life".*

can read the Gospel passage again, and then continue he meditation in my own way…

Ignatius Loyola, is:

http://www.jesuit.org/pilgrim/introgui.html

In the meditation, the Gospel references to being the light of the world and the Resurrection are not found in Mark but in John (8^{12}, 11^{25}).

(See also 'Day 14")

CTION

think today of four people who would care enough to ɔ out of their way to carry *me* and accompany *me*, ɔwering *me* down to Jesus. I pray for them and I also ray for those whom *I* would like to "bring" before the ord.

t another time I could reflect and pray in the same ind of way on one of the following passages:

The cure of a blind man – *Lk 18³⁵⁻⁴³*
The centurion's servant – *Lk 7¹⁻¹⁰*
The deaf and dumb man – *Mk 7³¹⁻³⁷*
Jairus' daughter raised to life – *Mt 9¹⁸⁻³⁶*
The man born blind – *Jn 9*
The ten lepers – *Lk 17¹¹⁻¹⁹*
The man with the withered hand – *Mt 12⁹⁻¹⁴*
The marriage at Cana: water into wine – *Jn 2¹⁻¹¹*

---

rtist Raymond Gaston has 'placed into the Gospel' (of is painting of the Marriage Feast at Cana: Jn 2¹⁻¹²) ɔme of his relatives and friends. The web-site also ɔows photographs of the people whose faces have een depicted:
ttp://www.culham.ac.uk/Curric/BBC/p3_instr.html

very extensive site about praying by 'placing self in e Gospel', based on 'The Spiritual Exercises' of St

Day 14   PRAYING FOR SOMEONE WHO IS ILL OR IN NEED

I relax,
call to mind God's presence,
and then pray for someone I know who is ill...

Loving Lord Jesus,
    we read in the Gospels
    that you spoke individually
    to many people,
    changing their lives
    as you showed them recognition and acceptance
    and as you brought them healing and wholeness.

We read, too,   *Mk 21-12*
    of how some people
    were such good friends
    of a man who was weak and paralysed,
    that they carried him on his stretcher:
    making their way through the crowds,
    carrying him on to the roof,
    and gently lowering him down,
    so that he could be right in front of you.
They must have been such good friends to him,
    and others could see
    the tenderness of their love and care
    as well as their extraordinary faith and trust
    in you, Lord,
    in bringing him into your presence.

And isn't it the very same
    that we are doing today, Lord
    – those of us who love and care for _____
    as we bring *her*, carry *her*,
    in the strength of our love
    into the warmth and light of your presence:
    knowing that you, too,
    are very fond of *her*?
We can all but hear you
    calling _____ by *her* name   *Is 431*
    as you are also calling *her* your friend,   *Jn 1515*
    and we know that your love never fails.   *1 Cor 138*

Lord,
    _____ – "the one you love
    – is ill" *(or in need)*,   *Jn 11*
    and those of us who join you
    in loving *her* and caring for *her*
    ask you to lay your hands on *her*   *Lk 440, Mk 52*
    and transform *her* life once again,
    bringing *her* the fullness
    of your healing and your life. Amen.   *Jn 101*

Accounts of children and teenagers with chronic illness
can be accessed at:
http://funrsc.fairfield.edu/ ~ jfleitas/contents.html

'Companion in Illness':
http://www.cptryon.org/prayer/heal/index.html

(See also 'Day 13')

Day 15   CALMING THE STORM

NEEDED

- *The Bible for the Gospel of St Mark and for a Psalm – or could access the Grail Psalms at: http://www.angelfire.com/il/psalter/*
- *A cushion.*
- *If helpful, I can access on the Internet the painting by Delacroix of the storm, 'The Sea of Galilee', via: http://www.southern.net/wm/paint/*
- *The song 'Do not be Afraid' on the CD/cassette 'Come Back to Me'.*

RELAXING

I can relax by closing my eyes and thinking of an occasion when I was on a boat or a ship, or was beside water.

(pause)

CALLING TO MIND GOD'S PRESENCE

I ask the Holy Spirit to lead me in prayer today…

I remind myself that Jesus is with me in the boat of my life. I can pray:

> **"Lord, the sea is so wide**
> **and my boat is so small.**
> **Be with me."**

(Prayer of a Breton fisherman)

(pause)

REFLECTING AND PRAYING

I read Psalm 107 (106) 23-32

It is often helpful when reading the Bible to *"place myself"* in the account being read. For example, in the account of Jesus calming the storm on the Sea of Galilee, I can picture myself as in the boat.

Chapter 4 of St Mark's Gospel (verses 35-41) tells of Jesus calming the storm. The Gospel (the Word of God) can be read whilst the book rests on a cushion, because today's Gospel passage will mention that Jesus (the Word of God) *"was asleep in the boat with his head on a cushion"*.

(pause to read Mark 4 35-41)

After reading the Gospel itself, the following words form a reflection or meditation, which I can pray slowly:

"I imagine myself in the boat with Jesus and other close friends of his, and a storm brews up on the inland Sea of Galilee. The day has been warm. I can still smell the salt water as well as the lingering odour of fish that have lain in the boat. I hear the birds that are disturbed by the sudden storm, and I see them fly off to the security of the land. I can feel the wind in my hair and a few drops of rain on my face. I see the white-topped waves as the wind scurries down the valleys that surround the Lake. I feel the disturbed, unsettling motion of the boat as the storm begins to toss it around – only a little at first, and then more menacingly – and I hear the growing waves smash against the side of the wooden boat. The sail makes a loud noise as the strong circulating wind makes it flap back and forth.

"Now the rain drives harder, and I hear the large drops strike the inside of the boat. What is normally a still and peaceful lake has become very disturbed and agitated. This is beyond my normal experience, and I know only too well that I am a poor swimmer, and the water here is deep.

"The gale reminds me of the storm within – the confusion and worries, the doubts and fears in my own life. As I look around in the boat, I see the faces of those who have become my friends. My fear is reflected in the anxiety shown in their wet and worried faces.

"Then I am surprised when I see that another figure – it is Jesus – not only is not bothered by the storm, but is actually asleep in the turbulent boat, and he even has his head on a cushion! I lean over and shake him to wake him up. He gives me that usual smile of his and looks directly into my eyes. I am surprised – but I think I'm also angry – and I say to him: *'Master, don't you care that we might sink?'* But then I realise it was a stupid thing to say, because I have often seen the personal care he has shown for individuals in many ways. Now I see him rub the sleep from his eyes, and then he stretches out his hand and commands the wind and the waves to be still – and so they become. I feel that tingling down my spine that I always feel whenever something extraordinary happens. I look around and see the same puzzled – and perhaps fearful – expression on the faces of my friends. Again, Jesus smiles and looks at each one in turn and says: *'Don't be afraid. What do you want me to do for* **you***?'* And I pause in silence for a while, thinking over those words he has just spoken: *'Don't be afraid. What do you want me to do for* **you***?' …"*

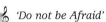 *'Do not be Afraid'*

ACTION

During the day I can pause to repeat the opening prayer or, if afraid, tempted, or anxious, I can turn to Jesus and say:

> **"Lord, save me!**
> **I'm sinking!"**

Or I could use the following words as a 'breathing prayer', saying the first line whilst breathing out, then taking the second line one or two breaths later – repeating the process at least several times:

> **"You stretch out your hand**
> **and save me, Lord."**
> *Ps 138⁷*

The Gospel passage and reflection could be put onto cassette and played back even whilst amidst water in a bath, or through earphones at night.

N.B. The question – *"What do you want me to do for you?"* is not found in this Gospel passage, but in Mark 10⁵¹.

Bishop Papias (about 140 A.D.) wrote that *"Mark, having become the interpreter of Peter, wrote down accurately, though not in order, all that he remembered of the things said and done by the Lord."* In a way that helps us place ourselves in the Gospel, Gerald O'Mahoney SJ (in his book, 'Praying St Mark's Gospel') re-words the whole Gospel to reflect Peter being present. Today's passage from Mark reads: *"Jesus was in the stern, asleep on the cushion and we woke him…"*

For views of the Sea of Galilee:
http://www.holy-land-online.com/tiberias/gallery.htm
or
http://www.jesus2000.com
(then select "Sea of Galilee")
or
http://www.mustardseed.net/html/pseagald.html

Photo of pilgrims seated on a hillside by the Sea of Galilee (with Beatitudes text):
http://www.angelfire.com/in/sanctuary/galilee.html

"UNLESS YOU CHANGE AND BECOME
Day 16 LIKE LITTLE CHILDREN..."

(Mt 18³)

NEEDED

- *It might be helpful to have a magazine photograph or picture of babies or young children – preferably with their parents.*
- *A child's game?*
- *The song, 'O Lord, your tenderness', from the CD/cassette, 'He Touched Me'.*
- *From the Internet I could download Rembrandt's 'The Little Children being brought to Jesus', via http://www.southern.net/wm/paint*

RELAXING

I can relax by thinking of some of the happy times in my own childhood and in that of children I may have influenced for good.

I might be able to play a game with a child or play a child's game, as a means of symbolically 'letting go' of some of the demands and stresses I might feel as an adult. As God 'takes on' my responsibilities, I become as 'happy as a child'. Jesus tells me not to be worried or afraid (Mt 6²⁵).

CALLING TO MIND GOD'S PRESENCE

I ask the Spirit to guide me in prayer today...

> 'The disciples asked Jesus, "Who is the greatest in the kingdom of heaven?" So Jesus called A LITTLE CHILD to him and set the child before them. Then he said: "Unless you change and become like little children, you will never enter the kingdom of heaven. And so the greatest in the kingdom of heaven are those who make themselves as little as this little child."'
>
> (cf Mt 18¹⁻⁴)

Visitors to Liverpool's Catholic Cathedral notice an unusual statue on ground-level: a statue of Jesus with young children. The artist, Stephen Foster, has so designed it that young children can climb and sit on flat 'stones' that are part of the statue and, indeed, people sometimes see that happening. It serves as a reminder that each of us can readily 'place ourselves' with Jesus in the Gospel.

I spend a few moments now in picturing myself present along with those I love, as Jesus gathers us to him, and he *"lays his hands on us and says a prayer"* (Mt 19¹³⁻¹⁵).

(pause)

REFLECTING AND PRAYING

I remind myself again of Jesus' words: *"Unless you change and become like little children..."*

> *"When Jesus urged people to repent, he was urging them to become as little children. He wasn't asking them to eat the dust. He was confronting them with the necessity of a radical change of outlook, a fundamental reorientation of their lives, so that they would no longer trust for security in the 'persona' they had built up – the drama of being 'me' which I continuously stage for my own benefit – so that they would no longer trust that, but have the courage to become as receptive as little children, with all the openness to life, the taking down of the shutters and the throwing away of the armour which that entails...*
>
> *"This is what repentance means: discovering that you have more to you than you dreamt or knew, becoming bored with being only a quarter of what you are and therefore taking the risk of surrendering to the whole, and thus finding more abundant life..."*
>
> H. A. Williams, 'True Wilderness'

What qualities of children might Jesus have had in mind in calling me to be *"like a little child"*?
- not anxious or troubled about the future
- trusting and completely dependent on their parents
- with a sense of being special

– joyful, with smiles and laughter
– curious to explore
– enthusiastic to learn and move forward
– loving and trusting
– powerless
– simple and innocent
– aware of surroundings
– readily influenced for good.

I reflect on each of these (and other) qualities in turn. I can word a prayer – either after each or on grouping two or three together – asking the Lord to help me to *"become a little child"*. For the first two qualities in the list, for example:

Lord Jesus,
    you told your friends
    not to worry about the future.   *Mt 6³⁴*
Show me – as you showed them –
    how to have the attitude
    of simple trust
    that young children have,   *Mk 10¹⁵*
    and place myself
    into the caring hands of our Father,
    just as I see the way my five-year-old niece
    looks at her parents…

In the touching book, *'Mister God, This is Anna'*, the young girl says to the author (Fynn):
'Ain't you gonna say your prayers?' 'Well, yes,' I replied, 'when I get to bed.' 'I want to say mine now with you,' she said. So we both got down on our knees and she talked while I listened.

I've been to church many times, and heard many prayers, but none like this. I can't remember much about her prayer except that it started off with 'Dear Mister God, this is Anna talking,' and she went on in such a familiar way of talking to Mister God that I had the creepy feeling that if I dared look behind me, he would be standing there. I remember her saying, 'Thank you for letting Fynn love me,' and I remember being kissed goodnight, but how I got to bed I don't know…

🎼 *I could play the song 'O Lord, your tenderness'.*

ACTION

On seeing a child today I will ask the Lord's blessing on that child, recalling that Jesus *"laid his hands"* on young children.

———————————————

The Internet has a site that reflects on *'The Prayer Jesus Taught Us'*, as we remember that he told us to pray as Jewish children would speak to their father: *'Abba'*:
http://www.cptryon.org/prayer/teach.html

The *'Our Father'* is given in 638 languages/dialects:
http://www.christusrex.org/www1/pater/index.html

The qualities of a child that Jesus may have had in mind come across clearly in Sister Wendy's book that is inspiring and touching for people of all ages: *'A Child's Book of Prayer in Art'*.

'Placing myself in the Gospel' can, in turn, lead me to be more perceptive of how integrated the Gospel can be in my daily life. Accordingly, Francis Thompson – in his poem, *'O world invisible, we view thee'* – writes of
    'Christ walking on the water,
      Not of Gennesareth, but Thames!"

Day 17 "I LOOK AT HIM, AND HE LOOKS AT ME"

Most of today's prayer is intended to be with few words: simply *"looking at him, whilst he looks at me"*.

NEEDED

- *Mark's Gospel*
- *For today's 'Action', the song 'Only a Shadow' from the CD/cassette, 'Come back to me'.*
- *An icon or another figure of Jesus, such as a crucifix. A suitable 'warm' icon would be 'Christ our Lord', a 16th Century icon from the Monastery of St Catherine, Sinai: http://www.ocf.org/OrthodoxPage/icons/data/pantokrator2.gif*

RELAXING

I close my eyes and think of some occasions when I 'knew' within – however fleeting a glimpse at the time – that I was really loved.

(pause)

CALLING TO MIND GOD'S PRESENCE

I pray that the Holy Spirit will lead me in prayer today...

I commit to memory these words of prayer, and then say them slowly several times:

**Lord, quietly and trustfully
I place myself
in your presence.**

(pause)

REFLECTING AND PRAYING

I take St Mark's Gospel and read of the encounter of the rich, young man with Jesus. I can focus particularly on the words:

*"Jesus looked steadily at him
and loved him."*

(Mk 10²¹)

I read Mark 10¹⁷⁻²²

St Teresa of Avila (1515-1582), emphasising the need to recognise God's presence, said:

*"The failure to realise that Someone is there,
that God is there,
lies in the root
of all our problems in prayer.
We will not do with him
what we expect others to do with us
when they speak to us
– **to look at him**."*

The same message comes across in the story of the French peasant who was often seen to spend time alone in a church:

*"What do you find to say
during those times alone?"
he was asked.
"I'm not alone," the man replied.
"I just look at Him, and He looks at me.
He's very fond of me, you know."*

I now set out to pray without a sense of needing to use words. Instead I can look at an icon or another figure of Jesus, or close my eyes and simply *'place myself next to Jesus'*, 'soaking up' his love.

(lengthy pause)

**Lord Jesus
you treasure
and hold a special place
for each and every person,
as though only that one individual exists,
and so I know that you accept me as I am,
in the reality of my life this day.**

May I grow in the faith
    that you look steadily at me   *Mk 10²¹*
    and love me tenderly   *Lk 15²⁰*
    and call me your friend.   *Jn 15¹⁴*

ACTION

A writer reminds us that
    "Prayer takes place in the heart
    rather than in the head."
                    (Carlo Carretto)

I will pause later in the day to *"look at him whilst he looks steadily at me and loves me"*. Looking at today's icon or another image (if it helps to do so) I can repeat slowly and over and over some words of Jesus, adding my own name:

    "I have loved you, (NAME),
    as the Father has loved me."   *(cf Jn 15⁹)*

An appropriate breathing prayer (see 'Day 15') might be:
    "Strong is your love for us/me, Lord;
    you are faithful for ever."   *(Ps 117²)*

Examples of praying through slowly repeating just a few words – e.g. *"Lord, have mercy"*, *"Draw me to you"*, *"Come, Lord Jesus"* – may be accessed on the Internet at:
http://www.osb.org/osb/cist/melleray/html/script8.html

Select 'Jesus in Art' on:
http://www.holy-land-online.com/

It was St John Vianney (1786-1859), the country priest, who engaged the French peasant in conversation.

JESUS AND THE FIVE LOAVES
Day 18   AND TWO FISH – gestures as prayer

NEEDED

- *St Luke's Gospel*
- *The hymn 'Here I am, Lord' from the CD/cassette 'He Touched Me'*
- *'The Miracle of the Bread and Fish' by Giovanni Lanfranco may be accessed on the Internet, via: http://gallery.euroweb.hu/index.html*

RELAXING

I sit in a comfortable position and close my eyes. I think of parts of my body in turn – shoulders, left arm, right arm, chest – focussing on the relaxing of muscles and the freeing from bodily tension…

CALLING TO MIND GOD'S PRESENCE

I pause to ask that I may be fully alive with the Spirit, asking him to pray in me…

I read Luke 9⁹10–17

As I have just read, Jesus
- *"made them welcome*
- *and talked to them about the kingdom of God*
- *and cured those who were in need of healing."*
I remind myself that he *wishes to do the very same with me*, too, and so I call to mind that he is with me…

1   **Lord Jesus,**
2   **I come before you now, just as I am,**
3   **with no pretence or show,**
4   **rejoicing in what is good,**
5   **and asking you**
6   **to transform with your healing touch**
7   **whatever may be negative in my life.**
8   **You took five loaves and two fish**
9   **to become more than enough**
10 **for many in need.**
11 **I give you my whole self**
12 **to be transformed**
13 **in your loving presence. Amen.**

REFLECTING AND PRAYING

As gestures may be very helpful in ordinary communication, hand gestures or whole-body gestures as well as posture may be aids in prayer, reflecting that I am approaching the Lord not only with my mind or my vocal cords, but with every aspect of who I am.

Sometimes my prayer might simply be by means of a gesture, such as raising by a few centimetres or more one or both hands (or a saucer or plate). This may represent an offering of myself and my situation, *to be transformed* – as did Jesus with the five loaves and two fish that fed over five thousand people.

I could take the prayer (above) once again and, in an unhurried way, use expressive gestures, e.g. (corresponding with the line numbers of the prayer):

1   Touching the wrist with one or more fingers: a sign that the deaf use for Jesus. Why?

2   Hands coming from the centre of the chest, outwards in an open gesture as the arms are spread wider.

3   Hands covering the face are moved to the side.

4   Hands touching the lips are moved outwards in an upward curve, revealing a beaming smile.

5   Outstretched arms.

6   A touch with one hand on the other, or repeating the touching of the upturned wrist.

7   The forefingers of both hands could be touching and then moved apart, making a wide negative sign.

8   Holding up five fingers of one hand and then two on the other.

9   Hands together in front can separate in an upwards and then sidewards gesture of enormity.

10 One hand outstretched horizontally (knuckles upwards) can be swept slowly from left to right over the 'crowd', whilst 'looking' at individuals 'in the crowd'.

11 Hands moving outwards from the centre of the chest, in an open gesture as the arms are spread wider.

12 Arms crossed over the chest may be opened out and extended.

13 Join hands in a gesture of prayer.

As such prayer aims to be personally expressive, it would be a contradiction if the 'mechanics' given here as an example were to become a hindrance in prayer. Individuals use whatever gestures are significant to them.

It would be helpful to *repeat this exercise slowly several times*, with whatever gestures are thought appropriate. Perhaps it becomes more personal as I spend time identifying with whatever gestures I use.

 I could play the hymn, 'Here I Am, Lord', praying with appropriate gestures to the words of the hymn.

ACTION

Symbolism itself can be my prayer. At odd, brief moments of the day ahead I can use various symbols. Even whilst others are around, no-one else need notice my discreet gestures of prayer e.g.

- Raising my hand a little as a prayer of offering.
- Putting my hand to my face and, with a finger or thumb, tracing a very small cross on my forehead.
- Putting two fingers on my upturned wrist to remind me of Jesus, whose love led to crucifixion.
- Fingers to feel the constant tireless pulse in the neck or wrist, reminding me of the never-ending love of God.
- Fingers touching my eyes: *"Lord, that I may see!"* (Mk 10[51])
- A hand touching my ear: *"Lord, that I may hear what you are saying to me."*
- A hand over the heart. Jesus wept when he heard of the death of his friend, Lazarus, and onlookers said: *"See how he loved him!"* (Jn 11[36])

Day 19   A HUNGER FOR JUSTICE

NEEDED

- *A piece of bread.*
- *The Gospel of St Matthew.*
- *The song 'Walk Humbly with your God' from the CD/cassette 'Holy One of Israel'.*

RELAXING

I rest in a comfortable position. With my eyes closed I keep a wide smile on my face for about a minute, which can be a practice that helps in keeping my personal circumstances in perspective.

CALLING TO MIND GOD'S PRESENCE

I ask the Holy Spirit to lead me in prayer…

Martin Luther King, the human rights activist, who would be murdered in 1968, said:
> *"Prayer is the most important thing in my life.*
> *If I should neglect prayer for a single day,*
> *I should lose a great deal of the fire of faith."*

Prayer and action have been compared to the two oars a person must use to propel a boat forward. If one oar is used exclusively on one side, the would-be rower makes little progress, but tends to go round and round. It is necessary to use both oars.

In the 8th Century BC, the prophet Micah said:
> *"Act justly,*
> *love tenderly,*
> *and walk humbly with God."*   (Mic 6⁸)

These profound words I can learn by heart. With eyes closed I repeat them slowly, over and over, as I call to mind that I am now *"walking with God"*: I am in his presence.

(pause)

REFLECTING AND PRAYING

I think of a couple of occasions when I have experienced or witnessed or heard about injustice.

(pause)

Isaiah is the longest book in the Bible. It comments on events between about 740 and 530 BC, during which time the people suffered as they were led away into Exile in Babylon (set around present day Iraq) before returning to their own land. Isaiah says:

> *"Cease to do evil.*
> *Learn to do good,*
> *search for justice,*
> *help the oppressed,*
> *be just to the orphan,*
> *plead for the widow."*   (Is 1 16-17: JB)

In St Matthew's Gospel is the mention of those who are hungry or thirsty, those who are strangers or need clothes, those who are sick or in prison. It is worth remembering that it is not only the 'bad goats' on the left of Jesus, but also the 'good sheep' on his right who do not recognise Jesus in their midst. Being considerate has become second-nature in those who are good, irrespective of whether or not they 'perceive' Jesus as present.

(I pause to read Matthew 25 31-46)

Helder Camara, (1909-1999), the Archbishop of impoverished San Recife in Brazil, once said:
> *"When I give food to the poor,*
> *they call me a saint.*
> *When I ask why the poor have no food,*
> *they call me a communist."*

I hold a small piece of bread in my hands and 'place myself' alongside those who suffer injustice, as I use the words of a Latin American prayer before meals:

**O God,
to those who have hunger, give bread,
and to those who have bread,
give hunger for justice.**

I take and eat the piece of bread. I pause to reflect in God's presence on how I can fulfil in my own life the words of the prophet Micah, about acting justly, loving tenderly, and walking humbly with God.

(pause)

♪ *The song, 'Walk Humbly', could be played.*

ACTION

At various moments in the day I can repeat to myself the words of the prophet Micah, which I have committed to memory, and consider the implications in my own life of those words.

———————————————

See also the prayer service of Day 23: *"Jesus alone in prison"*.

Articles on Justice issues may be viewed on the Internet at, for example:
'Columban Voices', a Justice Newsletter
http://www.columban.com/
and at
http://www.mcgill.pvt.k12.al.us/jerryd/cm/mainjus.htm

'The Common Good' is a very inspiring document on Catholic Social Teaching:
http://www.tasc.ac.uk/cc/cbc/cg.htm

CAFOD, the Catholic Fund for Overseas Development:
          http://www.cafod.org.uk/index.htm
Christian Aid   *http://www.christian-aid.org.uk/main.htm*
Fairtrade Foundation: *http://www.gn.apc.org/fairtrade*
Oxfam: *http://www.netecho.com/oxfam/*
Tearfund: *http://www.tearfund.org/*

The United Nations Commission for Refugees:
http://www.unhcr.ch/welcome.htm
The Saint Egidio Community:
http://www.italynet.com/st.egidio/egidio2.htm

See the author's book *'Praying Each Day of the Year'* for reflections about Matthew 25[31-46]: October 20 and 22.

Christ be beside me

Lead me, Lord,
to recognise you
in the person beside me.

http://tks.org/stpatrick.htm

Christ be before me

If I flew to the point of sunrise, Lord,
or settled at the farthest limits of the sea,
even there your hand would lead me;
your right hand would hold me fast.

Ps 1399-10

http://sailfish.exis.net/ ~ frimmin/Poetry/lorica.html

Christ be behind me

Lord, I commit my failures
as well as my successes
into your hands,
and I bring for your healing
the people and the situations,
the wrongs and the hurts of the past.

Give me courage, strength and generosity
to let go and move on,
leaving the past behind me,
and living the present to the full.
Lead me always to be positive
as I *'entrust the past to your mercy,*
the present to your love,
and the future to your providence'.

St Augustine

http://www.esa-online.org/een/html/stpatrick.html

Christ be below me

Lord, I rejoice
that nothing can come between me and your love,
even when I feel alone or in difficulty,
when in sickness or am troubled.
Even if attacked or afraid,
*'no abyss of mine is so deep
that your love is not deeper still'.*
Lord, you have experienced many hells of this world
but descended so that you can lift us up.
Be always near.

Rom 8³¹⁻³⁹

Corrie Ten Boom

http://www.byzantines.net/saints/st-patrick.htm#St. Patrick's Breastplate

Christ be above me

Risen Lord of life,
you not only died for us
but are now at the Father's right hand,
praying for us.

Rom 8³

http://sailfish.exis.net/ ~ frimmin/Poetry/loricapara.html

Christ in my sleeping

Lord, you mark when I walk or lie down;
all my ways lie open to you.
When I cease activity,
calm my mind.
When I am by myself,
be my companion and friend.
When I am weary and heavily laden,
may your Spirit renew me.
When I lie down, may it be in peace
for sleep to heal and refresh me,
for you alone, Lord,
make me dwell in safety.
Watch my sleeping,
guard my waking,
be always near.

Ps 1391-3

Ps 49

http://www.c3net.net/kennedy/breastplate.htm

Christ in my rising

Lord,
at the rising of your sun each morning
let the greatest of all lights
– your love –
rise like the sun
within my heart.

(from the Armenian Liturgy

http://www.acronet.net/ ~ robokopp/eire/ibindun.htm

From 'St Patrick's Breastplate'

I arise today, through God's strength to pilot me:
God's might to uphold me,
God's wisdom to guide me,
God's eye to look before me,
God's ear to hear me,
God's word to speak for me,
God's hand to guard me,
God's way to lie before me,
God's shield to protect me,
God's host to secure me.

http://www.wowzone.com/lorica.htm

http://episcopalnet.org/READINGS/PatrickConfesson.html

Day 20   IN THANKSGIVING

NEEDED

- *The song, 'Make us one, Lord', from the CD/cassette, 'Holy One of Israel'.*
- *Bible for the 'Action'.*

RELAXING

I sit comfortably, close my eyes, relax my body, and quieten myself within by simply focussing on the noises that I hear. I let a sense of peace grow within.

CALLING TO MIND GOD'S PRESENCE

I ask the Holy Spirit to lead me in prayer…

I call to mind that God is with me:
Blessed are you, Lord our God,
for being faithful to your people
down the ages,
amidst their faith and their lack of faith,
in their joys and in their sufferings.
I thank you that, like them,
you have also called me
and have chosen to be with me now…

REFLECTING AND PRAYING

The Jewish holy day, the Sabbath, starts on Friday evening. As family members gather together, the mother and then the father lead prayers that begin with the words, *"Blessed are you, Lord our God."*

Prayers on the Feast of Passover start in the same way and, on the day before his death, Jesus will have used those prayers at his last Passover, which became the first Eucharist (Mass). In the Eucharist today we use the same phrase in some of the prayers, as the bread and wine are raised at the Offertory.

Remembering that the word *"Eucharist"* means *"thanksgiving"*, I pause to give thanks to God for some of the people who have been blessings in my life, and for situations and events. I start each prayer with those same words:

Blessed are you, Lord our God, for…

(pause

Many Christians (and members of other religions) pause to pray before eating, reflecting on God's gifts, on those who have grown and prepared the food, on those who lack basic needs in our world, and in thanksgiving for (and blessing on) those who are about to share the meal and their friendship and love.

Such prayer reminds us of the inter-connectedness of all human beings. The poet, John Donne, reminds us that
   "No man is an Island, entire of itself;
   Every man is a piece of the Continent."

Instead of focussing on large food companies, I will think of the contributions of individuals who have their own families and concerns: people locally, nationally and overseas. As brothers and sisters, we all have responsibilities to one another. An international aid agency has used the phrase:
   "Live simply
   so that others may simply live."

𝄞 *The song, 'Make us one, Lord', could be played.*

I can join myself with others of many cultures across the world who will be praying at this very moment as they are about to eat:

God our Father,
   we thank you
   for the food that is before us,
   and for the friendship and company
   we experience.
We ask your blessing on ourselves
   and on those across our world

who have played their part
in growing and preparing
what we are about to share.
Open our hearts
to those both near and far away
who lack what we take for granted.
May we grow in your love
and always be thankful. Amen.

Another 'grace before meals' is:

**"For what we are about to receive
may the Lord
make us truly thankful."**

A custom in Germany and Austria is to pause in silence when first seated at a meal. In those brief moments before starting to eat, individuals may gather their thoughts and reflect and pray privately, giving thanks to God. Such brief moments in busy daily schedules can provide opportunities for God to *'slip in'*.

We need food but, to remind ourselves that we *"cannot live on bread alone"* (Mt 44), some people delay eating for a few moments (without others necessarily being aware of it) in order to pray. We need sleep, but some people arise a little sooner than they might prefer, in order to pray: sleep is essential, but praying is even more so. Moslems are invited to pray each morning as the muezzin cries from the mosque: *"Allahu akhbar" – "God is great; prayer is better than sleep".*

ACTION

I can consider pausing in silence for a few moments on certain occasions as a means during the busy day of allowing God to *'slip in'* e.g. on waking, before eating, before making a phone call, before going out.

I can also reflect on the words of St Paul:
*"For all things
give thanks to God."*   *(1 Thess 518)*

I could look up in the Bible Proverbs 1517 and 171

Day 21 **"DO THIS IN MEMORY OF ME"**

NEEDED

- *A small piece of bread (and, perhaps, some wine or grapes).*
- *Some gentle music for the relaxation period.*
- *The song, 'Make us one, Lord', from 'Holy One of Israel'.*
- *From the 'Web Gallery of Art' at http://gallery.euroweb.hu/index1.html can be accessed either (1) a wood carving (1498-1504) of the Last Supper from the High Altar of Toledo Cathedral: Use the site's Search Engine to select "Unknown Master – Spanish", and type as Search Text: "Last Supper", or (2) a painting of 'The Last Supper' by Jaume Serra, painted 1370-1400 (in Palermo).*

RELAXING

As I play some gentle music, I set out to focus on and relax parts of my body in turn…

I switch off the music.

CALLING TO MIND GOD'S PRESENCE

I ask the Holy Spirit to pray in me…

I can set out to place myself amongst the apostles as they sit down for the last Passover meal that Jesus will celebrate.

I find myself sitting almost opposite Jesus. I will be able to see the expressions on his face, and learn from the way he prays. I see him taking the bread and wine of the Passover meal, and he says:

> *"Take this, all of you…*
> *This is my body which will be given up for you…*
> *This is my blood which will be shed for you."*

And I hear what will be one of his last instructions:

> *"Do this in memory of me."*

This Last Supper has become the first Eucharist (Mass).

REFLECTING AND PRAYING

I place myself now alongside the millions of individual Christians who have celebrated the Eucharist over the last two thousand years:

- Christians before they met their death in the Colosseum in Rome,
- soldiers about to go into battle,
- for someone about to undergo a serious operation,
- at a wedding,
- in thanksgiving,
- for someone who has died in tragic circumstances,
- in the silence of a desert or on a hilltop,
- by a few people gathered secretly in the middle of the night in a concentration camp. Still today, some people risk their lives to celebrate the Eucharist.

(pause

The moon landing of July 1969 – as Neil Armstrong and Buzz Aldrin became the first people to walk on the moon – was one of the high points of human achievement. I can reflect, too, that Buzz Aldrin took with him to the moon some bread and wine that his local church had given him. Shortly after touchdown he thought of the first Eucharist as he prayed. He ate the bread and, in the moon's one sixth gravity, poured the wine into a small chalice. The very first food and drink consumed on the moon were the same as those chosen by Jesus at his Last Supper.

(pause

God our Father,
    if I could trace back
    through the last two thousand years,
    marking out routes from Jesus himself

and then through people
whose faith has touched others
and so reached me,
I would be astounded
by the individuals I would encounter.
I give thanks, Father,
for all those people throughout two thousand years
who have inspired others
and played their part in passing on
to generation after generation
the heritage of their living faith.
Especially I give thanks
for those who have lived their faith
through difficulties
and hardship and persecution.
I pray, Father, that I may grow
in your faith and love
through good times and bad. Amen.

Thinking of some of the very many places and situations in which the Eucharist has been celebrated, I join in spirit with others in prayer.

The hymn, 'Make us one, Lord', could be played.

ACTION

The word *"Eucharist"* means *"thanksgiving"*. I will take time to give thanks to God for much that is good in my life, and I will be careful to express my thanks and appreciation to others today in the ordinary events of daily life.

Reflecting on the Last Supper:
http://www.culham.ac.uk/Easter/link1.html

The scripture readings of each day's Roman Catholic Eucharist (Mass) can be accessed at
http://www.littleflower.org/slf/daymenu.htm
or
http://www.themass.org/
including audio excerpts of Sunday's intercessory

prayers and the homily), or
http://www.nccbuscc.org/nab/index.htm

'One Bread, One Body' – daily reflections on the scripture of the feastday and of any saint being commemorated:
http://www.veritas.org.sg/presentation_ministries/reflections/

Passover on the Net:
http://www.holidays.net/passover/
and at:
http://www.jcn18.com/holiday/passover/haggadah/intro.htm

Day 22   JESUS IN THE GARDEN

NEEDED

- *privacy to be able to lie flat on the floor for the second part of today's prayer.*
- *an olive (or something else that tastes bitter, e.g. horseradish).*
- *On the Internet, Mantegna's 'The Agony in the Garden' can be viewed at*
  http://sunsite.auc.dk/cgfa/
  and Giovanni Bellini's 'The Agony in the Garden' at
  http://gallery.euroweb.hu/index.html

RELAXING

I think of one or more enjoyable, relaxing times that I have spent in gardens or parkland.

CALLING TO MIND GOD'S PRESENCE

I ask the Holy Spirit to pray in me...

In poetic imagery, the Book of Genesis talks of God *"walking in the garden (of Eden) in the cool of the day"* (Gen 3⁸). Knowing how essential it is to focus on God's presence, I can reflect on these words:

"There should be in the soul
  halls of space,
  avenues of leisure,
  and high porticos of silence
  where God walks."   *(Jeremy Taylor, 1613-1667)*

I pause to call to mind that he is with me now.

                                        (pause)

REFLECTING AND PRAYING

I can set out to identify with Jesus in the Garden of Gethsemane on the Mount of Olives. The Last Supper is over, and he has walked in the evening air with his friends. He arrives at the Garden, with its age-old olive trees. His friends are physically with him – but they might as well not be, because they have fallen asleep – even though he had told them that he really needs them at this time.

It is a time of great stress, strain and pressure for Jesus as he faces the inevitable.

"The darkness you are encountering
  is in itself a rich experience.
If it be that you really want to meet our Lord,
  then it is by moonlight
  that you must seek him
  under an olive tree.
You will find him flat on the ground,
  and you will have to lie down on your face
  with him
  if you are to catch his words."   *(Hugh Kay)*

To help in placing myself beside Jesus at this time of difficulty, I could taste an olive (or something else that is bitter) as a reminder of the bitterness of the situation. In the same way, at the Feast of Passover, Jewish families taste bitter herbs. They are identifying with the bitter experiences of Moses and the people he led from slavery to the Promised Land.

I identify with Jesus in the Garden of Gethsemane. He knows he has yet to undergo much pain and suffering of many kinds. The Garden of the Resurrection is still a long way off (Jn 19⁴¹, 20¹⁵).

I can also place myself in the Garden of Eden in the passage from Genesis, the first book of the Bible. God says, *"Where are you?"* to the couple who are hiding. Today in the garden of *my* life, God asks, *"Where are you in your life? What's it all about?"* One way to help in facing those questions would be to lie flat on the ground beside Jesus in the Garden of Gethsemane. If appropriate I could now lie face down on the floor. My hands could be under my forehead, or stretched horizontally for my body to form the shape of a cross.

                                    (lying on the floor)

ising from the floor, I can pray:

ather,
    even amidst whatever difficulties I may face
    I rejoice that nothing can come between
    me and your love,
    even when I feel alone or in difficulty,
    when in sickness or am troubled.
ven if attacked or afraid,
    no abyss of mine is so deep
    that your love is not deeper still.

(based on Romans 8³¹⁻³⁹,
with the last two lines
being words of Corrie Ten Boom)

CTION

ater today I can learn these words of a psalm and,
ith eyes closed, repeat them slowly, over and over:

Out of the depths, Lord, I cry to you.
ord, hear my voice.   *(Ps 130¹)*

will think of and pray for others who will be
xperiencing feelings of isolation, rejection, separation,
eing abandoned, cut off, betrayed. How might I be of
elp to someone in such a situation?

Reflecting on the Agony in the Garden:
ttp://www.culham.ac.uk/Easter/link2.html

cenes of the Garden of Gethsemane/Mount of Olives:
ttp://www.mustardseed.net/html/pjrumold.html
nd some readings and prayers:
ttp://www.cptryon.org/xpipassio/medit/garden.html
nd also:
ttp://www.angelfire.com/in/sanctuary/sehwt2.html

Day 23   JESUS ALONE IN PRISON

NEEDED

- *The Gospels.*
- *An addressed envelope or postcard may help to focus my attention.*
- *The song, 'Such love', from the CD/cassette, 'Holy One of Israel'.*

RELAXING

I pause for a few moments with my eyes closed, resting in an inner quiet and peace.

(pause)

Our reflex action on bumping into something is to rub the affected part of the body. We realise that this tends to alleviate some of the pain. 'Massage' can increase the release of endorphins in the body (as does exercise), altering our experiences of pain, mood and hunger.

With each hand in turn, I slowly rub/massage first the fingers and then the rest of the hand. This may sensitise me to pain and the relief of pain – not only for myself but in thinking of the profound pain of different kinds that people are suffering now in 'prison' of body, mind or spirit...

CALLING TO MIND GOD'S PRESENCE

I ask the Holy Spirit to lead me in prayer...

I spend a few moments in silence, maybe in a different kind of *"aloneness"* from those who are held hostage or who are in prison or who are seriously ill, and I call to mind that Jesus is present with me.

(pause)

REFLECTING AND PRAYING

I can read John 18.12-19.16, which details Jesus being arrested and taken before the religious authorities and the state authorities.

(pause

 The song, 'Such love', may be played.

In his inspiring book, *'Taken on Trust'*, Terry Waite – the former special envoy of Robert Runcie, Archbishop of Canterbury – writes about his five-year captivity in Beirut, the capital of the Lebanon. He had gone there to try to negotiate the freeing of hostages, only to be taken captive himself.

One day, after four years of isolation, a guard handed him a postcard which somehow had reached him. It had been sent by someone he did not know – a well-wisher in Bedford – simply telling Terry that he had not been forgotten, and that many people were praying for his release.

On another occasion Terry was allowed access to a radio, and he happened to hear a religious service being broadcast from Belfast. Another person he did not know spoke of praying for all captives, and *"especially for Terry Waite"*.

As for Terry Waite, it may be encouraging in times of difficulty, to know that someone, somewhere, is praying for us. There are people in convents and monasteries who pray much of the day for people they will never meet. There are Christians who, in serious illness, transform their sufferings by offering them as prayer for the good intentions of people they will never meet. Many others – such as some who are living alone – make good use of their day in praying for others. Today I can pray for someone, somewhere, who needs the touch of God in their lives at this time.

God our Father,
   one of the greatest yearnings
   of the human spirit
   is to be free,
   and we know
   that there are many kinds of restriction
   that limit and confine us.
I ask that I may treasure
   the freedom that I have,
   and grow in sensitivity
   towards those
   who are less free than I am.
I join my prayer today
   with that of others
   who are praying
   for people they do not know. Amen.

ACTION

There are various ways of 'meeting' others – personally, on the telephone, in a letter, by e-mail. I can set out today to help lighten the burden of particular people I will meet: offering a smile, a cheerful word, some attention, and asking the Lord to bless them.

_____

Look at 'Courage' and 'Injustice' on:
http://www.culham.ac.uk/Easter/index.html

Mark's Account (and a commentary) on the Trial of Jesus before Pilate:
http://www.cptryon.org/xpipassio/passio/mark/5roman.html

Some web-sites on the Internet detail the abuse of human rights e.g.
Human Rights Watch: *http://www.hrw.org/*
Amnesty International: *http://www.amnesty.org.uk/*
Action on Human Rights:
http://www.bbc.co.uk/education/humanrights/
Human Rights, United Nations:
http://www.un.org/rights/

Day 24 CARRYING THE CROSS

NEEDED

- *The song, 'Walk humbly with your God' from the CD/cassette, 'Holy One of Israel'.*
- *The inspiring painting, 'The Procession to Calvary' by Pieter Bruegel the Elder, could be downloaded from the 'WebMuseum, Paris' at http://www.southern.net/wm/paint/*

RELAXING

I relax and 'centre' myself by focussing on each of my senses in turn, thinking of recent experiences with each: sight, hearing, touch, taste and smell.

CALLING TO MIND GOD'S PRESENCE

I ask the Holy Spirit to pray in me today…

I spend a few moments placing myself in the company of Jesus as he walks along the road towards Jerusalem. He knows that his journey of faith can end in only one way.

Reflecting with my senses may help in placing myself beside Jesus. I think, for example, of the *feel* of the hot air, the *taste* of the dust as some is blown into my face, the *touch* of the dry skin of my fingers, the *sound* of sandals on the dusty road, the *sight* of Jesus and the atmosphere he conveys.

(pause)

♪ *The song, 'Walk humbly with your God', could be played.*

REFLECTING AND PRAYING

Jesus has now spent his last few days in Jerusalem. He had been welcomed on Palm Sunday, celebrated the Passover (Last Supper), was betrayed, captured and condemned. Now he carries his cross as he walks the road to Calvary (Golgotha), the place of crucifixion. In my imagination I place myself beside him.

It would be helpful to have access to Bruegel's painting which vividly expresses the Incarnation – God being fully a human being – showing Jesus almost indistinguishable from the crowd of humanity.

Several times I can repeat in prayer Jesus' words to the Father:

> **"Not my will, Father,
> but yours be done."**
>
> *Lk 22*

ACTION

I can reflect during the day on the words of the poster: *'If you were arrested for being a Christian, would there be enough evidence to convict you?'*

'Stations of the Cross' may be viewed at:
http://www.christusrex.org/www1/jvc/index.html
and with Art at:
http://landru.i-link-2.net/shnyves/
(then selecting "Stations of the Cross").
Also:
http://www.cptryon.org/xpipassio/stations/index.html
and
http://www.dur.ac.uk/StChads/chaplain/stats.htm
and
http://www.osp.org.uk/worship/stations.htm

Day 25 SHARING IN THE PAIN

NEEDED

- *A cross or crucifix or icon of Jesus. Particularly appropriate might be looking at a crucifix by Cimabue, accessed on the Internet at:*
  http://gallery.euroweb.hu/html/c/cimabue/crucifix/index.html
- *Could make use of a medley of three hymns on the CD/cassette, 'He Touched Me': 'I love you, Lord/He touched me/He is Lord'.*

RELAXING

With eyes closed, I focus on my breathing, simply noticing if it is deep or shallow, fast or slow, through my mouth or my nose or both.

CALLING TO MIND GOD'S PRESENCE

I ask the Holy Spirit to inspire me in prayer…

A prayer that some people use (and is associated with the Orthodox traditions) is called *'The Jesus Prayer'*:

> Lord Jesus Christ,
> Son of God,
> have mercy on me,
> a sinner.   *(cf. Lk 18*[38]*, 17*[13]*, 18*[14]*)*

Some repeat the prayer slowly as a kind of 'breathing prayer': saying just one line at a time whilst breathing out, then saying nothing whilst breathing in: simply reflecting on the words just spoken. Either on the next breath out, or after a few breaths, the next line is spoken. It would be important to memorise the prayer so that it can be said either with eyes closed or looking at something like an icon of Jesus. This can be a very prayerful exercise if done slowly and repeatedly over several minutes, as a means of focussing on God's presence.

(pause)

♪ *The medley of hymns could be played.*

REFLECTING AND PRAYING

People who suffered the Roman execution of crucifixion, died from no longer being able to breathe. The pull downwards of the weight of their body diminished the capacity of their lungs. Victims could inhale only by pulling up with their hands (tied or nailed to the cross) and pushing down on their feet (which also were secured as a means of prolonging their agony). When the muscle pain became too great and they no longer had energy to move – the torture being such that it would last for hours – they died from suffocation.

Uncomfortable as it is to read those details, we know of suffering deliberately inflicted on people today – physical and mental suffering – as we see on TV and in the newspapers.

Father, in sympathizing with Christ on his cross,
> **we are sympathizing**
> **with suffering people everywhere.**
We are joining our prayers to the prayers of
> **the hungry and the thirsty,**
> **the hurt and the lonely,**
> **the sick and the dying,**
> **the outcasts and the refugees.**
We are uniting ourselves with
> **all who are oppressed,**
> **all the known innocents**
> **who are condemned to death,**
> **all who are betrayed by their friends.**
We are sharing in the pain
> **of all who are adjudged fools**
> **by the people they have served all their lives,**
> **all who are nailed to the cross**
> **of others' sins and stupidities,**
> **all who feel in their hearts**
> **that you, God, have abandoned them.**
We believe that Jesus Christ, your Son,
> **is also the Son of Man.**

We believe that in him all mankind
     has suffered, been humiliated and died.
But we are confident too
     that by his bruises all of us are healed.
This is why, Father, we take our place
     at the foot of his cross,
     knowing that Good Friday is really good
     because of him who loved us
     and gave himself for us.

(Peter de Rosa)

Whilst I could think of people I have seen on the news
or in the newspapers who are suffering, instead I will
focus now on some of the individuals I know. I pray for
them, knowing that they are 'Jesus' still in agony today:
     one who is scarred from the past, who carries hurts,
     someone with not long to live,
     a person who is lost without the person they love,
     an individual who has just been made unemployed,
     or who cannot get a job,
     one who feels inadequate,
     someone seriously ill,
     a person in mourning,
     one whose physical abilities are diminished,
     one whose mind is not what it might be,
     someone who struggles
     with the past, present or future,
     someone for whom life
     has lost any meaning or purpose…

CTION

can pray *'The Jesus Prayer'* again: slowly and
repeatedly.

More about *'The Jesus Prayer'* can be found on the
Internet:
http://www.goarch.org/access/orthodoxy/prayer
and
http://www.angelfire.com/in/sanctuary/jesusprayer.html

Reflecting on the Crucifixion:
http://www.culham.ac.uk/Easter/link7.html

Ten paintings from Palm Sunday to the Placing in the
Tomb, 'Behold the Man', may be accessed via:
http://www.ewtn.com/gallery/index.htm

'One People Sharing Christ's Passion' – reflections from
various countries:
http://www.christworld.com/world.htm
An icon (and text):
http://maple.lemoyne.edu/ ~ bucko/krivak.html

"JESUS, REMEMBER ME
Day 26   WHEN YOU COME INTO YOUR KINGDOM"

NEEDED

- *If possible, a recording of the hymn from Taizé: "Jesus, remember me" (to be found, for example, on the CD/cassette, 'Laudate: Music of Taizé')*
- *St Luke's Gospel*
- *Ruben's painting of 'Christ on the Cross' (with two thieves) may be downloaded from the 'Web Gallery of Art':*
  http://gallery.euroweb.hu/art/r/rubens/
  Then choose 'Religion' and 'Christ-C'.
  Rembrandt's drawing/cartoon of the Crucifixion is at:
  http://www.clark.net/pub/webbge/oct9804.jpg

RELAXING

I put my hand on my forehead and then, pressing quite firmly, I 'wipe' my face as I move my hand downwards. Each time starting at my forehead and working downwards, I spend a minute or so 'wiping' the rest of my face. It can be a means of alerting me to tension expressed in my face, as well as being a gesture of gentle attention to myself.

CALLING TO MIND GOD'S PRESENCE

I ask the Spirit to lead me in prayer today…

'Let us come into his presence
  whenever we can.
Let us try to imagine seeing the cross
  and him upon it.
Let us draw near.
Let us beg him to look on us
  as he did on the penitent thief,
  and let us say to him:
  "Lord, remember me
  when you come into your kingdom."'

(Cardinal John Henry Newman,
1801-1890)

REFLECTING AND PRAYING

I read from the Gospel: Luke 23[33-43].

I can imagine myself as the Good Thief, as I pray:

The more they spat and riled at him,
  the calmer he seemed to become.
I heard him say, above the noisy rabble,
  "Father, forgive them,
  they don't know what they are doing."
Then the other criminal on the cross
  started at him, too,
  and said something like:
  "Are you not the Messiah?
  Save yourself and us as well."
I knew nothing about a Christ Messiah,
  but that jibe was too much for me.
In the midst of my own dying pains
  I yelled at him to stop bawling at an innocent.
And I found myself saying to the middle-man:
  "Jesus, remember me
  when you come into your kingdom."

Loving Lord,
  you turned to me and managed to mouth:
  "I promise you,
  today you'll be with me in paradise."
Our eyes met, and I felt I'd known you all my life.
In the last hours of my life,
  I knew so much I'd never known before.
You learn quickly on crosses, or not at all.

(Denis Blackledge,
'Loving Lord: Encounters', pg 5

I play the Taizé chant, or simply repeat the same words slowly, over and over, being those spoken by the Good Thief on the cross beside Jesus *(Lk 23[39-43])*. If reciting the words, I can say the first line whilst breathing out, and then take the second line a few breaths later:

   "Jesus, remember me
     when you come into your kingdom."

(pause)

I can bring to Jesus on the cross my own concerns and worries, my burdens and hopes, my successes and failures. It might help in prayer to be able to 'visualise' this. With my hand in front of me at 45 degrees, palm downwards, I can appear to 'lift' something with my fingertips, and carry it to the foot of the cross, where I 'leave it', knowing that Jesus will 'take my burden' and will transform it. If words are helpful, I can pray those of the Good Thief, or:

All that I am, Lord,
I bring to you
to be transformed
in your presence.

(pause)

In the future, I can visually 'lift' and 'deposit' something whilst looking at a cross/crucifix/picture of Jesus from a distance, maybe simply saying: *"Over to you, Lord."*

ACTION

I can ask: *"What of myself do I lay on the altar?"* If helpful, I can memorise the following words of Albert Schweitzer (1875-1965), using them now and in the future, knowing that it can be useful to memorise such short prayers that will then easily come to mind at other times:

   "Here, Lord, is my life.
    I place it on the altar today.
    Use me as you will."

The web-site of Taizé, an ecumenical centre of prayer in southern France, is:
http://www.taize.fr/

Day 27 "FATHER, FORGIVE THEM; THEY DO NOT KNOW WHAT THEY ARE DOING" (Lk 23:34)

NEEDED

- *Pen/pencil and a piece of paper*
- *The song 'Lay your hands' from the CD/cassette 'He Touched Me'.*

RELAXING

I get into a comfortable position and close my eyes. I place my hands (whether upturned or down) on my knees for a couple of minutes.

(pause)

CALLING TO MIND GOD'S PRESENCE

I ask Jesus to breathe into me his Holy Spirit, and I ask the Spirit to pray in me...

I spend a few moments placing myself in the presence of Jesus who calls me by my name, touches me and smiles as he offers me forgiveness...

REFLECTING AND PRAYING

All of us – even the people we most admire – fall out with others from time to time. Walls can be built up, prejudices reinforced, and defensive positions consolidated.

Amidst negative feelings, it may be helpful to think of people who have suffered more than we have, yet have 'risen' to be able to forgive those who have done them very great harm. One such person was Gordon Wilson whose daughter, Marie, a nurse, lay dying beside him after a terrorist bomb exploded in Enniskillen, Northern Ireland. 11 people were killed on that day in November 1987. In words that touched many people across the world (and to which the Queen referred in her Christmas broadcast) Gordon Wilson said:

> *"I shall pray for those killers*
> *tonight and every night."*

Wisely, William Law (an 18th Century clergyman) stated that

> *"There is nothing*
> *that makes us love someone so much*
> *as praying for them."*

As a means to help me to pray for, love and forgive others, it may be helpful to *draw a circle* on a piece of paper. I can focus on that circle (which is never-ending, like a wedding ring) and so can be a useful symbol of the fullness of God's love, which is never-ending.

Into that circle I can write the names or initials of any people with whom I still have some difficulty of strained relationships. I can hold my hand over that circle in a symbolic way (if appropriate), as I pray for those people and for myself to be filled with the fullness of God's love, and experience his healing in our lives.

(pause)

𝄞 *The song 'Lay your hands' could be played.*

God our Father,
may no-one's negative actions
ever overpower my determination
to choose to live in a positive way.
I know that to forgive someone
can be far from being an easy option,
and I know that forgiveness
isn't somehow pretending
that something wrong hasn't happened.
Instead it is being generous, Father
– as your Son showed in his dying words –
in being willing to release the other person
from what natural justice demands
should be 'punishment' for wrong-doing.
Isn't this, Father,
what is meant by *"your mercy"*

and what *we* are to do
in being called
to *"be merciful"* ourselves?   *Mt 5⁷*

or what *I* have done wrong, Father,
forgive me
to the extent
that I am generous and gracious
in forgiving – or truly hoping to forgive –
those who have done wrong to me.   *Lk 11⁴*

Empower me
to break the cycle
of any hatred, resentment or bitterness,
always resisting evil   *Rom 12²¹*
and conquering it with goodness.

Bring your healing and peace and wholeness
into the lives of those I pray for,
and into mine. Amen.

ACTION

could memorise the words of William Law (here
expressed in inclusive language) which may then come
to mind in the future if difficulties arise with an
individual. May the words remind me to pray for and
love that person.

can reflect, too, on these words:
*"He who has been deeply hurt has a **right**
to be sure he is **loved**."*

Jean Vanier

_____

Gaugin's *'Yellow Christ'* can be viewed at:
http://www.clark.net/pub/webbge/jes09.jpg

The Crucifixion of Jesus':
http://www.cptryon.org/prayer/season/cross.html

Day 28   THE DIVINE RUBBISH-COLLECTOR

NEEDED

- *Some waste paper and a pen/pencil.*
- *A waste paper basket.*
- *The hymn, 'O Lord, your tenderness' from the CD/cassette, 'He Touched Me'.*
- *A crucifix or cross or icon of Jesus (e.g. as detailed in the Internet references on Day 17 or Day 1) or a simple cross drawn on a piece of paper.*
- *Two of many painted crucifixes can be accessed on the Internet at the Web Gallery:*
  http://gallery.euroweb.hu/index.html
  looking up 'Coppo di Marcovaldo' or 'Master of San Francesco Bardi'.

RELAXING

I can spend some time quietly relaxing and being still…

CALLING TO MIND GOD'S PRESENCE

I ask the Holy Spirit to fill me and burn within me…

With eyes closed, I spend a few minutes in peace and calm as I repeat to myself slowly these words from one of the psalms:

"Be still and know that I am God."   Ps 46¹¹

REFLECTING AND PRAYING

In 1986 the film, *'The Mission'*, was released. The setting is Brazil in the late 18th Century, as Spain cedes the area to the Portuguese. The character Mendoza (played by Robert de Niro) enslaves local people for the Portuguese.

In anger, Mendoza kills his own brother but Gabriel, a Jesuit priest (played by Jeremy Irons) saves him from killing himself. The guilt that Mendoza carries with him is represented by a large net which is full of swords and armour that he pulls behind him through the jungle. The burden is dragging him back and threatens his life as he tries to climb a perilous cliff. Only when the symbolic burden is released, does Mendoza discover himself and become free.

In a symbolic way I can lay before the cross of Jesus whatever burdens I am carrying – be they of sin, guilt, or difficulties. It may help to make use of the symbol of a crucifix or icon of Jesus, or to draw a simple cross on paper. I can use my fingertips to 'pick up' something invisible and then 'deposit' it (in the manner of a crane) in front of what is representing Jesus.

I might prefer to crumple up some sheets of waste paper, one at a time and slowly, and either throw them into a wastepaper bin or lay them before Jesus.

Loving Lord,
    you love all that you have made,   *Wis 11²*
    and it is your very nature
    to love and forgive and be faithful
    – no matter how unfaithful
    or unreliable I might be.
You tell us in the Bible
    that whatever wrong we have done,
    you tread down our faults
    to the bottom of the sea.   *Mic 7¹⁹*
We know there is no need
    to keep thinking
    about what we have done
    in the past,   *Is 43¹⁸*
    because you pardon
    the wrongs we have done,
    and you delight in showing mercy.   *Mic 7¹⁸*
You bind up all our wounds   *Ps 147³*
    and you renew us by your love.   *Zeph 3¹⁷*
Lead us to be generous and gracious
    in accepting and forgiving others
    in the same way
    as you accept and forgive us. Amen.

The song, 'O Lord, your tenderness', could be played.

Lord, I acknowledge my sinfulness.
I ask you to empower me
   with your Holy Spirit,
   that I may resist temptation
   and *"choose life
   rather than death"*,   *Deut 30¹⁹*
   – good rather than evil –
   in the ordinary circumstances
   of my daily life. Amen.

ACTION

From time to time in the day ahead, I can reflect on
these words:
   *"God doesn't make rubbish,
     but he does collect it!"*

                             (Damain Lundy, FSC)

Some short samples of monastic chant can be accessed
from *'The Monastery of Christ in the Desert'*:
http://www.christdesert.org/
on which I can select 'Chant'.
I could download the *'Kyrie' – 'Lord, have mercy'*, and
play it at the end of each of, say, three short petitions in
which I ask God for forgiveness for things that I have
done – or perhaps I could focus on my **attitude** which
tends to influence whether my words and actions will
be positive or negative.
The same site comments on the feastday.

Day 29 LAST WORDS

NEEDED

- *The song, 'Lamb of God' on the CD/cassette, 'Holy One of Israel'.*
- *For each of the "Seven Last Words", appropriate paintings may be accessed at 'The Web Gallery of Art':* **http://gallery.euroweb.hu/index1.html** *Then click on the appropriate letter of the artist's surname.*

1 *(Forgive)* – Bruegel, Pieter the Younger – Crucifixion.
2 *(Good Thief)* – Mantegna – Crucifixion.
3 *(Mother)* – Greco, El – Paintings between 1596-1600 – Retable of the Colegio Toledo – Crucifixion, Museo de Prado.
4 *(Deserted)* – Cranach, Lucas the Elder – Paintings: Religious – Crucifixion 1503; pine panel, Munich.
5 *(Thirst)* – Donatello – Late works – Crucifixion.
6 *(Accomplished)* – Grünewald – Isenheim Altarpiece – Crucifixion.
7 *(Commit spirit)* – Greco, El – Paintings between 1606-1610 – Christ on the Cross, Cincinatti.

RELAXING AND CALLING TO MIND GOD'S PRESENCE

I spend some moments in silence, relaxing my body and mind…

I ask the Holy Spirit to lead me in prayer and to bring me into the presence of Jesus…

REFLECTING AND PRAYING

The story of Abraham about to sacrifice his son, Isaac (Gen 22¹⁻¹⁴), tells us that God was not calling for human sacrifices (unlike the practices of neighbouring nations). Instead, Abraham sacrificed a ram, and the Jewish nation would continue to offer such burnt sacrifices to God in the Temple in Jerusalem. The very best was offered, at personal cost to the individual: no 'mangy' sheep – only the finest lamb! Those sacrifices,

though, could never themselves *'bring about'* a complete and total *'reconciliation'* and *'restoration of damaged relationships'* between God and humanity. Only a perfect sacrifice could do that and so, as God and humanity met fully in Jesus, he was the one whose personal sacrifice would restore perfectly the damaged relationship between God and humanity. Jesus was *"the Lamb of God who would take away the sin of the world"* (Jn 1²⁹).

 The song, 'Lamb of God' could be played.

In his sacrifice, Jesus (fully human) would bring all humanity with him (also being fully God) to God the Father, 'redeeming' or 'restoring' us to our 'rightful owner'.
"If Jesus Christ is not true God, how could he help us? If he is not true man, how could he help us?"
                                                Dietrich Bonhoeffer (1906-1945)

THE LAST WORDS
Special significance is often attached to a person's dying words. They may reflect the individual's life. Today's prayer is based around what are sometimes referred to as "the seven last words (phrases/statements) of Jesus". I can pray after each, possibly reflecting with the aid of the paintings listed above.

1   *Lk 23³²⁻³⁴*
As he is nailed to the cross, Jesus says:
"Father, forgive them;
    they do not know what they are doing."

2   *Lk 23³⁹⁻⁴³*
The Good Thief says to him:
"Jesus, remember me
when you come into your kingdom."
Jesus replies:
"I promise you:
    today you will be with me in paradise."

3   *Jn 19²⁵⁻²⁷*

To Mary, his mother, he says:
"Woman, here is your son,"
and to John the gospel-writer:
"Here is your mother."

4   *Mt 27⁴⁵⁻⁵⁰*

After three hours of darkness,
Jesus says:
"My God, my God,
  why have you deserted me?"   *(Ps 22¹)*

5   *Jn 19²⁸⁻²⁹*

When Jesus knew that all had been completed,
he said:
"I am thirsty."   *(Ps 22¹⁵)*

6   *Jn 19²⁹⁻³⁰*

After drinking the sour wine
that had been offered to him,
Jesus says:
"It is accomplished."

7   *Lk 23⁴⁴⁻⁴⁹*

The curtain in the Temple,
separating God's presence from the people,
was torn in two.
Crying with a loud voice, Jesus says:
"Father, into your hands
  I commit my spirit."   *(Ps 31⁵⁻⁶)*

ACTION

I could take one of the seven phrases and reflect on it
from time to time during the day ahead.

———————————————————

'Three hours, an eclipse, and 7 words':
http://www.angelfire.com/in/sanctuary/gf2.html

"LORD, WHAT DO YOU WANT ME TO DO?"

(St Francis of Assisi)

NEEDED

The meditation accompanies the picture of the Assisi crucifix on the opposite page.

I relax,
call to mind God's presence,
and then reflect and pray…

It was 800 years ago that Francis went to pray
in the run-down church of San Damiano in Assisi.
Unsettled, he prayed:
"Lord, what do you want me to do?"
He heard the voice of Jesus,
seeming to come from the painted crucifix:
"Francis, go and build up my Church
which is falling into ruins."
Francis set about re-building the chapel
with stones and mortar,
but gradually began to realise
that what he was being asked to do
was to build up the Church
– the community of God's people.

We can see on the crucifix
that below the arms of Jesus
are four angels, 'God's messengers'.
The twelve apostles are shown:
ten at the top of the crucifix,
and one beside each of Jesus' hands.
A cockerel near the bottom right of the crucifix
calls to mind Peter's denial of Jesus,   *Lk 22*34,54-62
reminding us also
that Jesus' love and forgiveness
embrace and encircle us
as much as they did Peter.   *Jn 21*15-17

Above Jesus' halo appear the Latin words
that are often abbreviated to
"I.N.R.I."
– *"Jesus of Nazareth, King of the Jews"*:
the words on the notice
that Pilate had fixed to the cross.   *Jn 19*19

The figure of Jesus rests on a black coffin;
he is the conqueror of death and sinfulness.
Blood is shown flowing from his wounds,

signifying his life flowing freely to all people.
In the red circle at the top,
Jesus is shown ascending to the Father,
whose right hand appears in blessing.
At the Father's right hand,
Jesus now prays for us.   *Rom 8*34

There are five large figures
next to Jesus on the cross,
and their names appear beneath them.
On the far left is Mary, the mother of Jesus.   *Jn 19*25-27
John the gospel-writer is next to her.
On the other side are Mary Magdalene,
Mary (the mother of James the apostle),
and the Roman centurion
(without a halo, and wearing a red cloak) who said:
"Truly this man was the Son of God."   *Mk 15*39

Several "little" people are also shown:
one is by Mary's feet,
another is by the centurion's feet,
and another peeps out
beside the centurion's head.
There are no haloes
to indicate that they are saints;
maybe one represents the artist himself,
and another the artist's patron.
Like them I can (in prayer)
place myself beside Jesus on his cross
because I, too,
am one of the 'insignificant ones',
one of the little ones
whom Jesus talks of in the Gospel:
"a little child", a "sparrow",   *Mk 10*13-16, *Lk 12*6-7
or "Zacchaeus",
the small person who is great
in God's eyes.   *Lk 19*1-10

The inspiring crucifix can be downloaded from a site that also gives further details:
http://www.empnet.com/stpauls/damiano.htm
and
http://www.capuchinfriars.org.au/sandam.html

Day 31   "LET LOOSE IN THE WORLD"   (John Masefield)

NEEDED

- *Either to be outside where nature's life is seen, or to be inside with a flower, plant, or bulb, or a picture of beautiful natural scenery (see the web-sites mentioned on Day 4).*
- *The Gospel of St John.*
- *If inside, the song 'I looked up' from the CD/cassette 'Holy One of Israel'.*

RELAXING

I look at what is around me – be it in natural surroundings outside, or with a flower in front of me, or looking at a scenic picture. I remind myself that what I see can be *"life-giving"* to me, depending on my attitude.

CALLING TO MIND GOD'S PRESENCE

I ask for the fullness of God's Spirit, asking him to pray in me…

Lord, you are not to be found
   in the emptiness of a tomb.
Instead, you are risen from the dead
   and present with me now
   as you promised to be.
I pause to remind myself that you are here,
   offering me your peace…

(Lk 24¹⁻⁸, Mt 28¹⁻¹⁰,
Mk 16¹⁻⁸, Jn 20¹⁻¹⁰)

REFLECTING AND PRAYING

I read a Gospel account of the Resurrection of Jesus: John 19³⁸-20¹⁸. The last part of Chapter 19 sets the scene, and that passage (19³⁸⁻⁴²) could be explored three times as, prayerfully, I 'place myself in the Gospel' – first as Joseph of Arimathea, then as Nicodemus, and then as Pilate…

The rest of the account is from Chapter 20, and I can meditate on it (20¹⁻¹⁸) firstly as Mary of Magdala (who thinks Jesus is *"the gardener"*), and then as Simon Peter. A third reading could be as John, the Gospel-writer himself (who coyly refers to himself as *"the one whom Jesus loved"* – cf Jn 13²³). I could read the passage a final time as one of the early Christians who had met Jesus before his death, but had not met him in person once Jesus was Risen from the dead: a Christian whose faith is of lived experience…

Loving Lord, we live in a resurrection-world.
That is faith-fact.
That is part of our human history and mystery.
Now that gets me rather excited!
Love changes everything –
   it even conquers death,
   and the terrifying power of Satan.
Through your real dying
   and your real rising
   you showed your love for us all –
   individually and as a community
   of sisters and brothers planet-wide.

Loving Lord,
   I want to try to put myself
   into the shoes of those individuals
   who lived through the strange privilege
   of being the first to see you really dead,
   then really risen.
I want to feel the sort of feelings
   they surely felt.

Let me feel their terror
   when they went to anoint a dead body
   and were faced by angels and aliveness!
Let me feel their fear,
   literally locked behind barricaded doors.
Let me feel their guilt,
   knowing they'd deserted
   the one to whom they'd promised
   their friendship and their following.

Let me feel their joy,
   almost too much to bear,
   almost too good to be true.

Let me feel their peace,
   your first resurrection-gift to all you meet.
Let me feel the overpowering sense
   of fresh freedom and future responsibilities
   written in your welcoming risen face.
Let me feel the intimate bonding
   from the bread and breakfasting   *(Jn 21 19-31)*
   shared with you, their risen Lord.

Let me feel that sense of urgency
   to spread this Good News,
   that sense of mission,
   of literally being sent by you
   to carry on your work.

Loving Lord, let me feel the Eastering,
   as you come to meet and greet me.
Amen.

(Denis Blackledge, SJ
in 'Loving Lord: Seasons')

🎼 *The song 'I looked up' could be played.*

ACTION

I will focus on what I can see and experience as life-giving, life-enhancing. In what ways can I be life-promoting today?

A 'breathing prayer' could be:
   "Lord I believe:
   help my unbelief."

(Mk 9 24)

Reflecting on the Resurrection:
http://www.culham.ac.uk/Easter/link9.html

The text of the Exsultet – a prayer that is sung or recited at the Easter Vigil – can be accessed at:
http://praiseofglory.alabanza.com/easter99.htm

Other sites relating to the Resurrection:
http://www.execpc.com/ ~ tmuth/easter/   and
http://www.cptryon.org/prayer/season/easter.html

NEEDED

- *To be in privacy indoors, in a place that is 'special' to me.*
- *Could make use of a medley of three hymns on the CD/cassette, 'Holy One of Israel': 'Open your eyes/See his glory/Reign in me'.*
- *If with access to the Internet, Holman Hunt's painting of 'Christ, the Light of the World' can be downloaded: http://metalab.unc.edu/cjackson/hunt/p-hunt5.htm*

RELAXING

I become comfortable, close my eyes, and think of something memorable in various rooms of my home. I think, too, of some ways in which I have helped make my 'house' into my 'home'…

CALLING TO MIND GOD'S PRESENCE

I ask the Holy Spirit to pray in me today…

I can stand just a few centimetres in front of a door that will open towards me. As a sign to myself of my dependence on God, I lean my head and possibly my hands against the door (being sure that it *does* open inwards!). I can reflect on this gesture of *"leaning on God"*, being fully dependent on him, and I call to mind that he is with me now.

(pause)

REFLECTING AND PRAYING

I can reflect on some words of Jean Vanier, who established the *L'Arche* communities for the mentally handicapped:

*"Prayer is to be in contact
with our own centre.
It is to be close to our own source.*

*It is to let Jesus make his home in us
and to make our home in him.
It is to be guided by Jesus,
our Good Shepherd."*

*(Jean Vanier
in 'The Broken Body', DLT)*

(pause)

The artist, William Holman Hunt (1827-1910), was criticised when his painting, *"Christ, the Light of the World"* was displayed in public. He depicted Jesus with a lantern in his hand, knocking in the dark on a door that had not been opened for a long time. The door was encrusted with weeds that were growing in front of it, and the hinges looked rusted because they had not been used.

The artist was criticised because he had forgotten – the critics said – to paint a handle on the outside of the door on which Jesus was knocking. Hunt explained that that was the whole point: the door could not be opened from the outside, only from the inside. Jesus cannot come within me unless I am willing to *"open the door"*.

In the delightful book, *'Mister God, this is Anna'*, we read: *'This is the curious nature of Mister God, that even while he is at the centre of all things, he waits outside us and knocks to come in. It is we who open the door. Mister God doesn't break it down and come in; no, he knocks and waits.'*

In a service of preparation for the Millennium, Cardinal Basil Hume stood before the symbolic 'Holy Door' of Westminster Cathedral and said: *"Let Christ into your life. Open up the door of your hearts. He is knocking. We are free to say 'Come in' or not."*

I recall, Lord, that you told your disciples
to go into their **"inner room"** to pray.   Mt 66
And so here I am, Lord,
in *my* "inner room",
my own special place.
Not only is it somewhere
where I feel comfortable

and can readily be myself,
but it serves as a reminder
to come to you in a genuine way,
just as I am,
with no pretence or insincerity
that only build up walls of separation
– whether with other people,
or with you.

Whenever I am anxious
   or afraid, Lord,   *Mt 6³⁴, Jn 14¹*
   or am not really myself,
   and *"the doors of my room are closed",*   *Jn 20¹⁹*
   do come and be with me
   and bring me your peace.

You told a friend to ask
   "Where is the room
   in which I can eat the Passover
   with my disciples?"   *Lk 22¹¹*
My answer, Lord, is *here*:
   because I am keen
   that there always be room
   in my life for you.   *Lk 2⁷*
As I hear you calling me and knocking,   *Rev 3²⁰*
   I open my door
   and invite you to come in,
   knowing that you are ready
   to join me, side by side.
As with any other guest in my home, Lord,
   I welcome you warmly,
   and I hear you say:
   "Make your home in me
   as I make mine in you."   *Jn 15⁴*

I could play the hymns on CD/cassette.

ACTION

Later today I can learn these words of a psalm and so
will be able to call them to mind in future. I close my
eyes and pray the words slowly, over and over:
   "In your house, Lord, shall I dwell
     for ever and ever."   *(Ps 23⁶)*

Day 33   WELCOME, LORD

NEEDED

- *To sit in a chair, with another chair beside or opposite.*
- *If required, a Byzantine mosaic of the face of Jesus could be accessed:*
  http://www.ewtn.com/gallery/holyface/hf21.htm
  or the face of Jesus from Piero della Francesca's 'Baptism of Christ':
  http://gallery.euroweb.hu/art/p/piero/francesc/baptism2.jpg

RELAXING

I remember the words of Jesus (Mt 6⁵⁻⁶) as he says that I should go into my own room to pray, and then shut the door and pray to our Father privately – avoiding any show or sham that might possibly take place when with others. "My own room" is a special place; it needn't be a place that I am the only one to use. It might even mean being somewhere peaceful in a car. For "own room" or "inner room" I understand the need to be alone and be truly myself, face-to-face with God: no pretence and no masks.

Asked what was most necessary for prayer, Martin Luther replied: *"Don't lie to God."* As I pray, I will set out *not* to pretend to be other than the person I really am, nor think that I '*should*' be saying particular things in prayer.

Wherever "my own room" is, I now relax in peace and quiet, thankful to be the person God has made me, however much I might need to grow.

(pause)

CALLING TO MIND GOD'S PRESENCE

I ask the Holy Spirit to guide me in prayer today…

I call to mind that God is present in this place. Is there anywhere, after all, where he is not?

(pause)

Julian of Norwich (1342-1420) wrote:
> *"Utterly at home,*
> *God lives in us for ever."*

(pause

Lord Jesus,
> you are risen from the dead,
> and the locked doors
> behind the fearful disciples
> could not keep you out.   *cf. Jn 20¹*
I ask you
> to unlock the door of my heart
> as I set out to pray.
I remember that you said
> that you call me your friend   *Jn 15¹*
> and you invite me
> to make my home in you.   *Jn 15*
Be with me as my friend
> and remind me
> that you are always with me.   *Mt 28²*

REFLECTING AND PRAYING

I place a chair either beside me or opposite me – in whichever place a good friend might sit with me. I imagine a knocking at the door. My prayer then can be of saying *"Come in!"*, realising that it is Jesus. I can gesture and invite him to sit down on the chair that I have provided. What expression is on my face? What is my 'body language' as Jesus sits beside me?

St Teresa of Avila (in Spain) recommended this way of praying, and added:
> *"Imagine Jesus at your side.*
> *Stay with this good friend*
> *as long as you can.*
> *You do not need to be concerned*
> *about conversation."*

My prayer will be of being with him as with a good friend. There will be times in my prayer when we will be silent, as we enjoy each other's company. There will be times when I put into words what I want to say. "Prayer," said St Cyril of Alexandria "is keeping company with God."

Orthodox Archbishop Anthony Bloom writes:
"The old lady said, 'These fourteen years I have been praying the Jesus Prayer almost continually, and never have I perceived God's presence at all.' So I blundered out what I thought. I said, 'If you speak all the time, you don't give God a chance to place a word in.' She said, 'What shall I do?' I said, 'Go to your room after breakfast, put it right, place your armchair in a strategic position that will leave behind your back all the dark corners which are always in an old lady's room, into which things are pushed so as not to be seen. Light your little lamp before the icon that you have, and first of all take stock of your room. Just sit, look round, and try to see where you live, because I am sure that if you have prayed all these fourteen years it is a long time since you have seen your room. And then take your knitting and for fifteen minutes, knit before the face of God, but I forbid you to say one word of prayer. You just knit and try to enjoy the peace of your room."

Later the old lady reported that all had gone well, adding that she had said to herself: 'Oh how nice; I have fifteen minutes during which I can do nothing – and without feeling guilty!' She said that she came to appreciate her surroundings more, and discovered that the silence she discovered was not simply an absence of noise. The silence around met the silence within her, and she experienced the presence of God.

praying, and discover which suits me well. It will probably be the case that different postures can reflect different ways of praying. Dr Sheila Cassidy talks of clasping a mug of tea and sitting cross-legged on the floor in front of an icon and a candle. She even uses a large hour-glass which she turns upside down, illustrating her 'abandonment' of herself to God for an hour: the busy doctor being willing to 'waste time' "keeping company with God".

At various times and according to particular circumstances and feelings, some individuals sit cross-legged on a bed with their back to the wall, keeping the spine vertical. Others may kneel (often with the spine kept upright). Some stand or walk or sit in a comfortable chair (with hands resting on the knees or lap) or in a hard-backed chair with hands on the table. Some may pray in the bath or shower, or lie on the floor face-up or face-down.

ACTION

I can spend moments later in the day, growing more aware that the ordinariness of my place of prayer can also reveal the splendour of God's presence.

During the day I can make use of the 'Jesus Prayer' – see Day 25.

Over the next few days I can try various postures for

Day 34   JOURNEY TO EMMAUS

NEEDED

- *The Gospel of St Luke.*
- *The song 'Walk Humbly' on 'Holy One of Israel'.*
- *Caravaggio's painting, 'The Supper at Emmaus' can be accessed on the Internet via 'The WebMuseum, Paris': http://www.southern.net/wm/paint*

RELAXING

I can pause to think about an enjoyable and exciting journey in which I learned something about myself.

CALLING TO MIND GOD'S PRESENCE

Lord Jesus, yours is not
   the emptiness of a tomb.
Instead, you are risen from the dead
   and present with me now.
Fill me with your Spirit
   and help me to grow closer to you as I pray.

REFLECTING AND PRAYING

Using a CD-ROM of the (Jerusalem) Bible, search facilities readily extract passages throughout the Bible that mention, for example, *"journey"* or *"walk"*. The following prayer was written in that way, 'weaving' together some of the passages. The two themes of *"walking in God's presence"* and being called to undertake a *"journey of faith"*, come together perfectly in the Gospel passage of the Risen Jesus appearing to two disciples on the road to Emmaus, which I will read later.

God our Father,
   the images of *"journey"*
   and *"walking in your presence"*   *1 Sam 230*
   are vivid throughout the Bible.

We read
   that you walked in the Garden of Eden
   in the cool of the evening.   *Gen 38*
Many good people
   – like Noah, Abraham and Isaac –
   were said to *"walk with God"*.   *Gen 69,2440,4815*
Amidst famine in the land of Israel,
   Jacob's sons journeyed to Egypt
   to obtain grain,
   and there met their brother, Joseph,
   whom they had abandoned.   *Gen 425*
Four hundred years later
   you used Moses to lead your people
   to walk through the sea   *Ex 1416*
   from slavery in Egypt.
You watched over them
   at every stage of their forty-year journey
   as they made their way
   to the Promised Land,   *Ex 4038*
   feeding them with manna.
Four hundred years later still,
   your prophet Elijah was strengthened
   by the food that angels brought him:
   strengthened to walk
   for forty days and nights
   to the place
   where you wanted him to go.   *1 Kgs 198*
Isaiah prophesied
   that the people who walked in darkness
   would see a great light,   *Is 91*
   and those who put their trust in you
   would walk and never tire.   *Is 4031*
In the fulfilment of this
   and of *all* prophecies,
   Jesus, your Son, came amongst us,
   and those who now follow him
   do not walk in the dark:
   they have the light of life.   *Jn 812*
It was whilst walking,
   that Jesus called Levi, the tax-collector,   *Mk 214*
   and Simon and Andrew, the fishermen.   *Mt 418*
Later, Jesus would walk to them on the water
   as they were sitting in a boat.   *Mt 1426*
Tired by another journey,

Jesus met the Samaritan woman at the well
and confided in her
that he was the Messiah.   *Jn 4²⁶*
When criticised by some scribes,
Jesus replied: *"Which is it easier to say:*
'Your sins are forgiven'
or 'Get up and walk'?"   *Mt 9⁵*
and the man strode away,
healed both of his sin and of his disability.

Father, you call us to walk wholeheartedly
in your ways.   *2 Chron 6¹⁴*
Guide us on the journey we undertake,   *1 Sam 9⁶*
and show us
how to avoid being overburdened
on the pilgrimage of faith and service
that you call each of us to make.   *Mk 6⁸*
Teach us your ways
so that we may walk in your path,   *Is 2³*
following Jesus, who is the Way.   *Jn 14⁶*
Lead us to walk beside him,
faithfully and humbly. Amen.   *Ps 86¹¹, Mic 6⁸*

This prayer explored the matching themes of *"walking
in God's presence"* and being called to undertake a
"journey" of faith. Praying reflectively may have helped
to offer insights into the Gospel passage I am about to
read. Luke tells of the risen Jesus appearing to two
followers during their journey to the village of Emmaus.
I can place myself in the Gospel account, particularly as
I may see it as reflecting my own journey of faith e.g.
positive experiences in faith, disillusionment, deeper
personal understanding, growth in faith…

(I pause to read Luke 24¹³⁻³⁵)

♪ *The song 'Walk humbly with your God' could be*
played.

ACTION

Later today I will return to the prayer about *"walking in
God's presence"* and my *"journey of faith"*.

Day 35   RENEWING MY COMMITMENT

NEEDED

- *A lit candle (or a torch), recalling the symbol of the candle given for each person at baptism (christening), and of the Easter (Paschal) Candle that is also lit at the time of baptism.*
- *The song 'Peace like a River' from the CD/cassette 'Holy One of Israel'.*

RELAXING

I spend a few moments in silence, being aware of the warmth of the candle, the light it sheds, and any noise the flickering flame may make.

(pause)

CALLING TO MIND GOD'S PRESENCE

I ask for the warmth and light of the Holy Spirit as I set out to pray…

 The song 'Peace like a River' could be played.

Lord, may this candle and its gentle light
   remind me
   that you choose to be with me now
   as I pray:
   you who are
   the light of the world.   *Jn 8:12*
Like the disciples who met you
   on the road to Emmaus   *Lk 24:13-35*
   after you had risen from the dead,
   so, too, may *my* heart burn within me
   with the warmth of your presence.

(pause)

REFLECTING AND PRAYING

There are some thought-provoking scenes in Francis Coppola's film, *'The Godfather: Part II'*, about a Mafia family. Michael Corleone stands at the baptismal font, acting as godfather to a young relative. As he replies on behalf of his godchild, saying *"I do"* to each of the baptismal promises, the camera shifts after each question to one of several gruesome murders being committed at that very moment on the orders of Michael Corleone.

I could reflect in prayer on each of the baptismal promises, or could make use of the following *'Act of Dedication'* proclaimed by the young people at Ninian Park, Cardiff, in the presence of Pope John Paul II during his pastoral visit to Great Britain in 1982:

Do you believe in God the Father?

We do believe. We accept God as Father and origin of life; creator and designer of all things. He is the source of all beauty and power, who supports his people in justice and truth.

Do you believe in God the Son?

We do believe. We accept Jesus as the Christ, the Son of God, our brother and redeemer. He is our crucified and risen Lord, the Way of faith, the Truth of hope, and the Life of love.

Do you believe in God the Holy Spirit?

We do believe. We accept the Spirit of God as the giver of life, the bond of unity and peace. He is the spirit of wisdom, the fire of perfect love who renews our minds and hearts.

Do you resolve to be God's People today and tomorrow?

We do resolve. We promise to listen to him in the community of the Church, to follow his ways and live in his love.

Do you resolve to live as God's People today and tomorrow?

We do resolve. We promise to respect all life as God's gift to us, to protect the right to life, and to promote especially the dignity, worth and wonder of each human person.

Do you resolve to share together your life as God's People, today and tomorrow?

We do resolve. We promise to recognise all people as our brothers and sisters, to resist prejudice based on race, creed or colour; to seek ways of living in harmony, unity and tolerance.

Do you resolve to work as God's People today and tomorrow?

We do resolve. We promise to co-operate in our work with God's creative design, to defend the right to useful and satisfying work, to share the results of our labour, our possessions and our resources.

Do you resolve to seek peace as God's People, today and tomorrow?

We do resolve. We promise to be peace-makers in the world in which we live; to turn aside from war and violence; to build God's Kingdom where the poor and disadvantaged find hope and true justice.

ACTION

Later in the day I can return to a phrase from the *'Act of Dedication'*.

Day 36   FATHER, SON AND SPIRIT

I relax
and then remind myself that God is with me.

(pause)

Some Christian traditions make use of the *'Sign of the Cross'* as a gesture and prayer of trust, offering and commitment. It is a reminder of the price of loving that Jesus paid, but it can also be a means of recalling the Trinity, the three Persons in one God.

With the fingers of my right hand
I touch my forehead:

> **In the name of the Father**

With my fingers on my chest:

> **and of the Son**

With my fingers to my left shoulder
and then my right:

> **and of the Holy Spirit. Amen.**

I can make the Sign of the Cross more slowly as I reflect on each Person of the Trinity:

In the name of the FATHER
> **whose fingers formed the universe**
> **and whose love brought me into being,**
> **who sculpted me in my mother's womb**
> **and calls me tenderly by my name.**

In the name of the SON
> **– fully God yet also fully one of us –**
> **Jesus of Nazareth and of everywhere,**
> **risen from the dead:**
> **calling me his friend,**
> **inviting me to follow him,**
> **laying his hands of healing upon me.**

And in the name of the HOLY SPIRIT,
> **who hovered over the waters as creation began:**
> **the breath of life,**
> **the living bond of love,**
> **the giver of vision,**
> **inspiring, enabling and transforming.**

ACTION

With a finger I can draw a cross on my forehead, praying in words that may be used on Ash Wednesday, as many Christians are marked with ashes on their forehead:
> **"Turn away from sin**
> **and believe that God loves you."**

I may find it helpful to trace a small cross on my forehead or heart before I go to sleep, and as soon as I awake in the morning.

At other times of the day a small cross may be traced on the forehead or on a hand (no-one need notice) as a reminder of God's presence, and as a prayer of trusting in God's Providence – such as when starting work, before eating or driving, when in a difficult situation…

Recalling the symbolism in Baptism and Confirmation, I can dip the tip of my thumb in a little olive oil (or oil used for cooking) and then trace a cross on my forehead. Oil is a sign of the strength and empowering of the Holy Spirit.

For *'The Sign of the Cross'*:
http://www.cptryon.org/prayer/sign.html

"MADE IN THE IMAGE AND LIKENESS
Day 37   OF GOD"

(Gen 1²⁶)

NEEDED

- *A mirror positioned in such a way that I can see my face reflected back.*
- *Could make use of a medley of two hymns on the CD/cassette, 'Come Back to Me': 'When I feel the touch/Jesus, take me as I am'.*

RELAXING AND
CALLING TO MIND GOD'S PRESENCE

I breathe in and then form my lips as if to pronounce the letter "O" as I breathe out. As I keep repeating the exercise, may the sense of cleansing breath remind me to cleanse my inner self.

Knowing that I am the *"temple of the Holy Spirit"* (1 Cor 6¹⁹) I ask the Spirit to pray in me now...

"Prayer essentially is to become present
  to oneself, to God, to all reality...
We are so caught up
  with the events and the people in our lives
  that we rarely take time
  to consider our own selves
  to be worth any time at all...
The closest reality to God
  that one will ever experience
  is oneself.
Each of us is an existence of God,
  a presence of Christ,
  a Sacrament of the Church,
  a gift to the world."

Edward J Farrell,
'Celtic Meditations', Dimension Books

I think over these words and relax in the comfort of God's love for me, reminding myself that he is with me now.

(pause)

REFLECTING AND PRAYING

"Remember that you were made
in the image and likeness of God.
And so you should love yourself,
recognising your own beauty
*as a **mirror** of God's beauty."*

(Hildegard of Bingen,
1098-1179)

I spend time thanking God for the person he has made me...

♪ *I can play the medley of songs:'When I feel the touch/Jesus, take me as I am'.*

I ask forgiveness for whatever is not as it might be...

I pray that the Spirit moulds and transforms me more and more into the image of Jesus...

Lord Jesus, light of the world,   Jn 8¹²
  as the moon reflects the light of the sun,
  and as this mirror reflects
  what is before it,
  so may your light shine in me.
Then, however dimly,
  may others see your image and reflection,
  and so come to know you
  for themselves. Amen.   Jn 4⁴²

ACTION

I can set out in the early morning to read again the quote of Hildegard, and then look in a mirror and smile at myself for at least 15 seconds. This initial positive outlook may be of help in influencing my attitude (and others' attitude) throughout the day. Smiling is also known to lower the levels of stress.

I will look for God's image reflected in the people I will meet today, especially in people I may not particularly like. Doing so will probably affect my attitude, behaviour and words to them.

Day 38   PRAYING ABOUT MYSELF THROUGH WRITING

NEEDED

- *Pen/pencil and paper.*
- *Some symbols of myself – either the symbols themselves or a drawing of them, possibly in the form of a badge or heraldic shield, maybe with a motto added. The symbols may represent my hobbies, interests, my background, family members, family name, things that have happened to me... Alternatively I could focus on what I would choose to take with me (other than people and animals) if fleeing from a fire at home.*
- *A blank cassette and recorder for the 'Action'.*
- *'Yahweh, I know you are near' from the CD/cassette 'He Touched Me'.*

RELAXING

When in a comfortable position I close my eyes. As I become quiet within, my breathing will probably slow down, as will my pulse...

CALLING TO MIND GOD'S PRESENCE

I ask that the Holy Spirit who lives within me will lead me in prayer...

Slowly and repeatedly I say:
"Father, you search me and you know me."   *(Ps 1391)*

♪ *'Yahweh, I know you are near' could be played.*

REFLECTING AND PRAYING

I can set out to pray in *writing* today. I can look at the various symbols that I have chosen that say something about me, and then I name them on paper. I can jot down a few points about each of the symbols.

For example, the choice of a gardening tool might give rise to the following points:
- the life and vitality plants give me
- a sense of peace, quiet and harmony
- a skill I have picked up from a particular person
- the ability to enjoy myself, and 'enjoy enjoying' myself!

At times we express various kinds of prayer, including
- sorrow, regret, requesting forgiveness
- praise, adoration, worship
- thanks
- offering
- intercession, requests, petition.

Will I want to address my prayer to God the Father (Creator), Jesus (especially if referring to the Gospel), or the Holy Spirit who inspires and empowers?

Taking the example of focussing on a garden tool, I could write some words which I could draft and alter a few times, until I feel that they best "reflect me". An advantage in doing this will be that, at times when words won't come easily to me in prayer, I can return to these and pray "with myself". Such prayers also form a kind of 'personal journal' of my growing relationship with God.

A personal prayer (regarding a gardening tool) might end up something like this:

God our Father,
I've many happy memories of my uncle
who taught me all I know about gardening.
His enthusiasm was contagious!
I thank you for everything about him
and especially for his love of life
that he passed on to me.
I think, too, of the life and vitality,
the beauty and the inspiration
that plants give to me and to others.
I am creative when I garden,
and I can sense
sharing in your own work of creation.

I think, too,
    of how I can work quietly and peacefully
    and, after a few hours,
    I know that I gain
    a better sense of balance in my life.
May the friendship of others in the allotment
    remind me always to respect and value
    all who come into my life.
I thank you for all these good things
    which remind me of your own goodness.
I offer myself to you,
    like the fruits of the earth at harvest-time.
I pray, too,
    that I may sow and nurture fine things
    for others to enjoy. Amen.

ACTION

I could speak some prayers on to a cassette tape, whilst keeping a written/printed copy (or a list) of them. At other times I will then be able to play the cassette and "pray with" someone with whom I can *identify perfectly* in accent, pronunciation, emphasis, feeling, intonation, pitch, natural speed, age, gender, background, experience etc. This can be a very helpful way of praying, and the cassette might be played to good effect in the future, be it on a Walkman or in a car, or via headphones during a sleepless night.

Which prayers could be used? Some from this book could be recorded, or from other prayer books. Some psalms could be taken e.g. Psalms 8, 23, 25, 34, 51, 63, 65, 67, 84, 91, 103, 104, 113, 117, 130, 138, 139, 145, 147. The very readable *'Grail'* version of the Psalms is at:
http://www.angelfire.com/il/psalter/

At first it will be necessary to read the prayers whilst playing the tape, but some of the prayers in time will become at least partly memorised.

Collections of prayers are also available on the Internet e.g.
http://ireland.iol.ie/ ~ adi/prayers.htm

Day 39 BECOMING WHAT I HAVE IT IN ME TO BE

RELAXING AND 'FOCUSSING'

Perhaps unlike some other hosts of television 'chat shows', Oprah Winfrey is known to inspire others and bring out the best in those who are present for her programmes. Despite having suffered physical and sexual abuse when a child, she is a remarkable person who, through the quality of her life, conveys to others that, with help, they too can make it through whatever problems they face. We can break the cycle of evil, fear and hatred, we can be healed, and we can come through the experience in such a way that we are strengthened to help others.

Interviewed by Michael Parkinson in February 1999, Oprah said that, before any show starts, she takes the opportunity of travelling in the lift to "centre" herself, and ask God to "use her" in whatever way he wants during the time ahead.

I close my eyes, relax my body and mind, and focus on the present moment...

I ask God to use me in whatever way he wants during the time ahead...

I ask the Holy Spirit to pray in me...

CALLING TO MIND GOD'S PRESENCE

Lord Jesus,
   you tell us
   that the kingdom of God is amongst us. *Lk 17²¹*
Lead me now
   to grow more aware of your presence.

REFLECTING AND PRAYING

William Barclay wrote:

*"There are so few people
   who become what they have it in them to be.*

*It may be through lethargy and laziness,
   it may be through timidity and cowardice,
   it may be through
   lack of discipline and self-indulgence,
   it may be through involvement
   in second-bests and byways.
The world is full of people who have never realised
   the possibilities which are in them.
We need not think
   of the task which God has in store for us
   in terms of some great act or achievement
   of which everyone will know.
It may be to fit a child for life;
   it may be at some crucial moment
   to speak that word and exert that influence
   which will stop someone ruining life;
   it may be
   to do some quite small job superlatively well;
   it may be something
   which will touch the lives of many
   by our hands, our voices or our minds.
The fact remains that God is preparing us
   by all the experiences of life
   for **something**;
   and the fact remains
   that there are so many
   who refuse the task when it comes,
   and who never realise that they are refusing it."*

('The Gospel of John', Vol 1
Saint Andrew Press. Pg 40

I pray that the Holy Spirit "frees" and "opens me up" so that I may really see and hear, perceive and understand. I pray that he show me both how to live the present moment to the full and how to move ahead with my life in the power and freedom and joy that the Spirit brings.

The following prayer was found on a piece of wrapping-paper beside the body of a woman in the Nazi Concentration Camp of Ravensbruck, where 92,000 women and children were killed:

"O Lord,
   remember not only
   the men and women of good will,
   but also those of ill-will.
But do not remember
   all the suffering they have inflicted on us.
Instead, remember the fruits that have come to us
   thanks to this suffering:
   our comradeship, our loyalty,
   our humility, our courage,
   our generosity,
   and the greatness of heart
   which have all grown out of this.
And when they come to judgement,
   let all the fruits that we have borne
   be their forgiveness."

(pause)

"Life is to be lived
by striking a line
through every minus
and turning it into a plus."

(Elizabeth Kubler-Ross
'Death: the Final Stage of Growth' pg 230)

I pause to think briefly about some of the 'negative' times in my life, and focus on some of the strengths of character and other positive elements that grew out of those situations, remembering as I pray that it's not so much what happens to us, but what we *do* with what happens to us…

Carry out a random act
of seemingly senseless kindness,
with no expectation of reward or punishment
– safe in the knowledge that, one day,
someone somewhere might do the same for you."

I could list some random acts of kindness others have made towards me recently e.g. someone unknown holding open the door for me, and I can think of such acts of my own in the last few days.

Especially for those unable readily to meet others, acts of kindness can include praying for individuals and families selected randomly by opening a telephone directory and pointing a finger. Similarly, a street plan or atlas may be opened.

Random Acts of Kindness
http://www.udayton.edu/~ csc/randomacts.html

A web-site – 'Random Acts of Kindness' – details relevant text from an Oprah Winfrey Show:
http://www.intouchmag.com/oprah.html

See also Day 2.

ACTION

Princess Diana said:
"Perhaps we're too embarrassed to change,
or too frightened of the consequences
of showing that we actually care.
But why not risk it anyway?
Begin today.

Day 40   LOVE CHANGES EVERYTHING

NEEDED

- *The song 'Lord, you are so precious to me' from the CD/cassette 'He Touched Me'.*

RELAXING

I place my hand on my heart or on my wrist or the side of my neck, to monitor my pulse. As I focus on relaxing in peace and quiet, my heartbeat is likely to slow down.

(pause)

CALLING TO MIND GOD'S PRESENCE

I ask for the fullness of the Holy Spirit, that he may pray in me today and empower me to live as the person I am called to be...

With my hand on my heart – the heart often being thought of as a symbol of love – I call to mind how overwhelming is God's love and fondness for me, and I rejoice that I am in his presence.

(pause)

REFLECTING AND PRAYING

A popular choice at weddings is this scripture passage from St Paul, writing in about 57A.D. to the Christians in the Greek city of Corinth. I read it slowly and reflectively:

*"**Love** is patient and kind.*
***Love** is not jealous*
or boastful, or arrogant.

*"**Love** is respectful of others*
and does not look for selfish advantage.
***Love** is not touchy or resentful.*

***Love** takes no pleasure*
in the wrongs of others,
but rejoices in all that is good and right.
***Love** is always ready to excuse others.*

*"There is no limit to **love's** vision*
and commitment and faithfulness.
When all else fails,
***love** is there."*   *(1 Cor 12³¹⁻¹⁴)*

These words, surely, are a description of JESUS himself, as we remind ourselves that *"God is love"*

(1 John 4¹⁶)

Now I take Paul's words again, reading the name ***"Jesus"*** in place of the word *"love"* each time. I can reflect on how each phrase might call to mind some incidents in the Gospel e.g. how Jesus was *"respectful of others"*, was *"ready to excuse others"*, and remained *"committed and faithful"*, etc.

♪ *'Lord, you are so precious to me' could be played.*

I can pray through the passage a third time – now putting in **my own name** instead of *"love"*. How accurate a description – a 'photo-fit' – of myself are those words? I could think of instances in which I lived out some of those phrases, and occasions when I did not...

I can pray through each phrase of the passage a final time, asking the Lord to *enable me* to become what I couldn't become simply *by my own efforts*. My prayer could start like this (which is set around the first paragraph of St Paul's text):

*"**The things, good Lord, that I pray for,***
* **give me your grace to work for.**"*
At the same time
** I ask you to enable me**
** to become what I couldn't become**
** simply by my own will and efforts.**
So I ask you
** to empower me with your Spirit**

that I may grow more patient and kind,
    especially when...
I know that, in asking these things,
    opportunities will come my way
    for living out
    what I am praying for!
Lead me not to be
    jealous of the talents or possessions of others.
Instead...

ACTION

Several times today I could pray the following words
which could be committed to memory for future use:

"Most merciful Redeemer,
    Friend and Brother:
    may I know you more clearly,
    love you more dearly,
    and follow you more nearly,
    day by day."

They are words of St Richard of Chichester (1197-1253),
and were popularised in the song, 'Day by Day', in the
musical 'Godspel'.

I will be aware today of opportunities to live out the
good things I have been praying about.

The main prayer started with some words of
St Thomas More (1478-1535).

Day 41   IMAGES OF GOD

NEEDED

- *'Yahweh, I know you are near' from the CD/cassette, 'He Touched Me'.*
- *A touching image of God the Father was presented by Jesus as he told the story of the Prodigal Son (Luke 15¹¹⁻³²). The warmth of that image is seen in Rembrandt's 'The Return of the Prodigal Son', painted about 1662, which can be accessed on: http://www.southern.net/wm/paint/*

RELAXING

Once in a comfortable position, I close my eyes and focus first on relaxing the muscles in my shoulders, and then gradually in turn the muscles in my neck, face, arms, hands, legs and feet.

CALLING TO MIND GOD'S PRESENCE

I ask the Holy Spirit to inspire me and lead me in prayer…

(pause)

Father and lover of life,
   you know the depths of my innermost self,
   and you understand me.
You protect me on every side,
   shielding me from all harm.
When you put me together
   in my mother's womb,
   you knew all about me.
I thank you for the wonder of myself,
   and I stand in awe
   at all that you have made.
As you know and love me,
   so may I come to know and love you.
Guide me in your ways.

(based on Ps 139)

The hymn, 'Yahweh, I know you are near', could be played, which is a setting of the same psalm.

As is emphasised throughout this book, the key element in prayer is growing in awareness of God's presence. I pause to do so now.

(pause)

REFLECTING AND PRAYING

Thoughts of God as "Father" are likely to differ between someone whose experience is of genuinely loving parents who have warmly encouraged and invited the growth of their child, and someone whose lived experience is of a parent who had difficulty expressing love, or a parent who was indifferent or neglectful or abusive. For some of us, various feelings – such as childhood guilt, apprehension, fear or unhappiness, or being uncomfortable in a parent's presence – influence in a negative way our perception and experience of God himself. And so we may be reluctant to spend quality time with God in the silence that prayer often is (and needs to be). Instead of the scriptural *"Speak, Lord, your servant is listening"* (1 Sam 3⁹), I may be changing it into *"Listen, Lord, your servant is speaking!"*

Our images/ideas of God are also influenced by what we have read and been told and, of course, according to what others convey in being positive or otherwise in living out their lives as Christians. And so the image that *people* convey, can cloud the way that others picture and experience *God* to be.

Gerard Hughes writes:

"Our notion of God is mediated to us through parents, teachers and clergy. We do not come to know God directly. If our experience of parents and teachers has been of dominating people who show little affection or respect for us as persons, but value us only in so far as we conform to their expectations, then this experience is bound to affect our notion of God, and will influence the way we relate to him…

"Although I may know in my mind that God is not like that, I may still experience a strong disinclination to approach him, without knowing why, and find a thousand reasons for not praying – I am too busy, I prefer to find him through my work, etc. We have to pray constantly to be rid of false notions of God, and we have to beg him to teach us who he is, for no one else can. 'God is known by God alone', as one of the early writers of the church said. What we are praying for is not merely an intellectual knowledge, but a felt knowledge which affects our whole being and therefore affects the way we see ourselves, other people, and the world around us. This felt knowledge of God changes the patterns of our thinking and therefore of acting, breaks open the cocoon of our minds and hearts, and liberates us from the constrictions which our upbringing and present environment are imposing on us.

"To become aware that we have a distorted notion of God is to have made progress on our journey towards him. As the journey continues, we shall discover other distortions of which we were not aware. Such discoveries can be very painful at first, but it is like the pain we feel when our limbs are at last set free after being constricted; it is the pain of freedom. The journey to God is a journey of discovery, and it is full of surprises."

Gerard Hughes, SJ
'God of Surprises'

Yahweh God,
  you alone,
    can change the false notions I have of you:
    many thoughts from my own experience
    of which I may now be unaware.
Reach deep within me and liberate me
    from whatever may distort
    your true likeness.
Bring me back – time and time again –
    to Jesus, your Son,
    in whose attitude and words and actions
    I can see clearly
    your perfect image.

Col 1 15

In his *'Return of the Prodigal Son'*, Rembrandt paints the repentant son with his shaven head against the father's chest: reminiscent of a newly-born baby being held with its head against its mother. The father's cloak appears womb-like to encompass the child. The hands of the father rest on the shoulders of the son and are painted quite differently: one appears 'masculine' and the other 'feminine'.

To whatever degree I might focus on 'feminine' and 'masculine', an inspiring and moving passage in Isaiah can help me to appreciate the *'fullness'* of God's love:

"Can a woman forget her baby
or fail to cherish the child she bore?
Even greater is my love;
I will never forget you.
See, I have written your name
on the palms of my hands."

Is 49 15-16

ACTION

Will I let God touch me, kiss me, love me?

With some similar themes to Psalm 139, Francis Thompson's poem, *'The Hound of Heaven'* is at: *http://www2.bc.edu/ ~ anderso/sr/ft.html*

Day 42   "THERE IS A VARIETY OF GIFTS"

NEEDED

- *Pen/pencil and paper.*
- *The song, 'Holy Spirit, we welcome you', from the CD/cassette, 'He Touched Me'.*

RELAXING

Once in a comfortable position, I close my eyes and slowly blow out of my mouth as my lips form the letter 'O'. I then close my mouth and inhale through my nose, and repeat the process several times. As I breathe out slowly in the way mentioned, I can imagine tensions leaving my body, mind and spirit. I breathe in with a slow deep breath, and I picture all that is life-giving coming into every part of my body, mind and spirit.

CALLING TO MIND GOD'S PRESENCE

Many radio waves are travelling about me at present, but I am not aware of them until I use a radio to 'tune in' to them. Likewise I need to 'tune in' to focus on God's presence. I use a *breathing-prayer* as I 'tune in' to him, breathing out as I say one line, then reflecting and praying on those words as I breathe in. The idea is to know the words by heart, so that there is no need to look at the printed page. When ready, I move on to the next line:

Holy Spirit, breathe your life into me!

Holy Spirit, breathe your power into me!

Alternatives, as appropriate, might be to substitute "light" and "peace", or simply to pray repeatedly:

"Holy Spirit, come and live in me!"
or
"Holy Spirit, be fully alive in me!".

REFLECTING AND PRAYING

I ask Jesus to breathe into me the fullness of his Holy Spirit, that he may lead me in prayer...

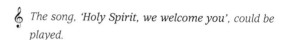 *The song, 'Holy Spirit, we welcome you', could be played.*

Some of the GIFTS of the Spirit are listed in Isaiah 11 1-3, and this prayer focusses on each of them:

Lord, I pray for the Spirit's gifts of *knowledge*
   and *wisdom* **and** *understanding.*
I pray for the ability
     to make *balanced judgements* **and choices,**
     and for the *courage* **then**
     to do what I realise I am called to do:
     courage to defeat the obstacles
     of fear and uncertainty,
     and courage to give me strength
     and determination and perseverance.
May your Spirit lead me
     to have great *respect and reverence*
     for all creation, for each person,
     and for you, my God.
Open my eyes in *wonder and awe*
     at all that is around me,
     so that all that I see
     may lead me to grow in awareness
     of your love and your presence.

Played at the funeral of the human rights activist, Martin Luther King (1929-1968), was a recording of a sermon he had preached just a short time before he was assassinated. His own voice was heard, stating that he hoped that – at his own funeral – someone would be able to say that he did try to feed the hungry, give drink to the thirsty, welcome strangers, clothe the naked, and visit the homeless and those in prison (cf. Mt 2531-46).

One way of reflecting on how well I may be using my God-given talents, is to think of what people might say about me in a sincere way at my own funeral.

Whatever approach I decide to take, I now make a list
of some of my gifts, talents, special abilities – thanking
God for them, and for how others have been blessed
through them.

(pause)

Lord, you have enriched my life
    in many ways.
Show me how best
    to use the time and talents and opportunities
    that you give me,
    so that I may give in service to others
    the good gifts I receive from you.
Lead me to be both humble and generous
    in praising others
    for the good use of their talents
    – looking not so much
    at the degree of achievement,
    but at the effort put in.
May your Spirit empower me
    to work well with others
    and bring out the best
    in those you have placed into my life.

ACTION

Today I will look for others making good use of their
gifts, talents and special abilities, and I will take
opportunities to encourage and praise them, and show
appreciation.

'Pentecost: The Holy Spirit comes':
http://www.cptryon.org/prayer/season/pentecost.html

Day 43   BEARING FRUIT IN THE SPIRIT

NEEDED

- *Pen/pencil and paper.*
- *Either the song, 'Peace like a river' from the CD/cassette 'Holy One of Israel', or 'Holy Spirit, we welcome you' from 'He Touched Me'.*

RELAXING

I can go outside and take some deep breaths of fresh air. I return to my place of prayer and there, closing my eyes, I simply monitor my breath as it slows down and possibly becomes more shallow.

CALLING TO MIND GOD'S PRESENCE

One of the images used of the Holy Spirit is that of WIND or BREATH – necessary for us to live. I can reflect that direct contact (such as by mouth-to-mouth resuscitation) refreshes, renews or brings new life. The wind is like the Spirit because it is strong and invisible. As with windmills, the Spirit brings power, enabling us to do what we could not do simply by ourselves.

With these images in mind, I breathe in slowly and then, as I breathe out, I say:

Come Holy Spirit!

The next time I breathe out, I say:

Come, fill my life!

Over a few minutes I repeat this 'breathing prayer', preferably with eyes closed.

REFLECTING AND PRAYING

Unlike in many other languages, nouns in English are neither masculine nor feminine, but neuter: we refer to a knife or fork as "it", whereas in French, for example, a knife is considered masculine (le couteau) and a fork as feminine (la fourchette).

In Greek the Holy Spirit is neuter: *it*. In Latin the Spirit is masculine: *he*. In Hebrew the Spirit is feminine: *she*. In the Early Church the emphasis (based on the Hebrew) was on the Holy Spirit as feminine, influencing people's perception of the Three Persons of the Trinity: Father, Son and Spirit.

 The hymn could be played.

Endowed with GIFTS of the Holy Spirit (cf. Is 11 1-3) and *"rooted"* firmly in Jesus (Col 2 7), each of us will *"bear fruit"* (Jn 15 5). It may help to sketch a tree on a piece of paper with the name 'Jesus' written across its 'roots', and some named fruits growing from its branches. Some 'FRUITS' – results of the Spirit being 'alive' in me – are: **love, joy, peace, patience, kindness, goodness, trustfulness, gentleness, and self-control** *(Gal 5 22).*

I can set out to pray to the Father about each of these **fruits of the Spirit** in turn.
I might
- think of how Jesus used or talked about it;
- think of how someone I know shows that fruit in their daily life;
- ask for forgiveness or healing regarding an occasion when I didn't live in that positive way myself;
- ask that the Spirit inspire and empower me to live more fully in that way.

For example, with *'trustfulness'*:

Father, I remember that Jesus
encouraged children to be close to him,
and he told the adults around them
that they should be as trusting in you, Father,
as young children are in their own parents.

can see that kind of look of trust and dependence
  in my young nephew
  when his mother bends over his pram,
  and it is touching to see how his tiny hand
  grasps my little finger!
thank you, Father, for the witness of trust
  shown by Ian and his parents.
ay that spirit of trustfulness grow with him.
can think of situations in my own life
  when I failed to have real trust
  in those who have loved me.
ask for your healing in any situations of the past
  that might still tend to hold me back
  from being as trustful as I might be.
ask for your blessing
  and for the power and inspiration of your Spirit
  that all of us may live more fully,
  bearing good fruits
  from the many gifts you have given us.
ead us to bring out the best in one another.

can now focus my prayer on some of the other
RUITS of the Spirit – love, joy, peace, patience,
ndness, goodness, gentleness and self-control. I can
erbalise my prayer or write it down, ready for use
gain in the future, whilst remembering that the task is
› pray rather than to produce a written composition.
ome people find it helpful to return to their written
ayer and adapt it further for future use.

CTION

can pray later in the day about another gift of the
pirit.

"IN THE NAME OF JESUS,
Day 44   I WILL GIVE YOU WHAT I HAVE"

NEEDED

- *The New Testament.*
- *It would be helpful to have the hymn 'Lay your hands' on the CD/cassette 'He Touched Me'.*
- *For the 'Action', some pictures from newspapers that show people – particularly if they are in need. It is also possible to access such pictures on the Internet e.g. "Picture of the Day" in LIFE magazine: http://www.pathfinder.com/Life/ or on BBC News Online': http://news.bbc.co.uk/ or http://www.skynews.co.uk or http://www.washingtonpost.com/wp-srv/photo/galleries.htm or the 'Lead Photo' in 'Yahoo': http://www.yahoo.co.uk/*

RELAXING

When in a comfortable position I put my hand on the top of my head. Pressing quite firmly I 'stroke' my head, repeatedly bringing my hand downwards, so that every part of my head has been 'stroked' firmly. Slowly I do the same with my neck and shoulders, and then with my arms and hands, and at least with my upper body...

I spend some moments in inner quietness...

CALLING TO MIND GOD'S PRESENCE

I ask the Holy Spirit who dwells within me, to lead me in prayer today...

Lord Jesus, we read in the Gospel
   that all those with friends who were sick
   brought them to you,
   and you healed them.   *Lk 440*
I place myself now in your care,
   and I ask you to lay your hands on me
   and bring your healing and wholeness,
   so that I may live more fully
   in your presence.

As you look warmly at me,   *Mk 1(*
   lead me to be genuinely loving
   in the way I treat myself
   as well as others:
   you who "heal the broken-hearted
   and bind up all our wounds." Amen.   *Ps 14*

♪ *I could play the hymn, 'Lay your hands'.*

REFLECTING AND PRAYING

I now read from the Acts of the Apostles:
Chapter 3, verses 1-16, which mentions the phrase,
"Silver and gold have I none, but what I have I give you.
the name of Jesus Christ..."

(paus

At the death in 1999 of Cardinal Basil Hume, many public figures commented that it was not so much wh. he said or did that influenced people, but that he showed forth the presence of God. *"When he came in, the room lit up as if a thousand lights had been turned on"*. Cardinal Hume himself wrote:

> *"In our public life we move further and further away from God and the things of God, and yet in the heart of men and women I believe that the yearning for Go is becoming more and more intense.*

> *"When the first apostles went out into the streets of Jerusalem at the first Pentecost, they had nothing material to give to the poor and needy. "Silver and gold I have none", said St Peter, "but what I have I give you; in the name of Jesus of Nazareth, walk." Th crippled man, his handicap cured, went leaping into the Temple in order to praise God.*

> *"The towns and cities of our land are full of people who do not need our silver and gold, but desperately need to hear the Good News of the Gospel. They are lamed and crippled without God. They perish because they do not have any vision about life and its meaning, and about the right way to find happiness. They need to know, they need to experience, that ther is a God who loves them...*

"The worst poverty today is the poverty of not having spiritual values in life. It is more crippling than material poverty. We Christians have to realise just how much we have to give, simply because we are baptised... We have within us a power to do wonderful things for God. We have the proud name of Christian; we are followers of Christ; we belong to him. Why is it then that we so often lack confidence? Why do we think we are helpless? In the meantime the city of man goes on its way hungry, and in a sense lost.

*"We live in a world where so much has been achieved. Our generation knows how to put men on the moon, but does not know the meaning of life. It looks to the people of faith for help. But often we remain silent, uncertain how to respond. We have to cure that lack of confidence. How do we do it? The answer is simple but very demanding. We need the inspiration of the Spirit; we need to speak about God as people who know him, as people who have seen the invisible. **It can only happen if we learn to pray**."*

(Cardinal Basil Hume:
'To be a Pilgrim', pp 47-48)

'Spiritual reading' can be more than a matter of picking up good ideas or finding some inspiration. In the passage above I can now take each paragraph or few sentences in turn and see how the words apply – not to others – but to myself. It is important to have time for silence. I then turn to God in prayer before moving on to the next section to be read.

ACTION

I can take time to look at and reflect on one or two evocative pictures in newspapers (or on web-sites named above) that reflect the joy or the suffering and pain of others. I then pray for the people and situations concerned. If the symbolism is appropriate, I can stretch out a hand towards the photographs that represent the people I am praying for.

Day 45   THE SPIRIT PRAYS IN US

NEEDED

- *A New Testament.*
- *Pen and paper.*
- *'Holy Spirit, we welcome you' from 'He Touched Me'.*

RELAXING

I close my eyes and relax as I think of some occasions when others' love and care and concern for me were 'visible' and tangible…

CALLING TO MIND GOD'S PRESENCE

Many people find it very helpful to pray for the inspiration of the Holy Spirit before they start to read a passage from the Bible, and I do so now, whilst calling to mind his presence:

Holy Spirit,
    I believe that the Christian Scriptures
    were inspired in a special way by you,
    and written by God-filled people
    who reflected on their encounters with Jesus
    in their own lives.
As I am about to read the Word of God,
    I ask you to be with me and inspire me.

'Holy Spirit, we welcome you' could be played.

REFLECTING AND PRAYING

Having read a scripture passage, many people read the words more slowly for a second time. On the third reading of it, the words can be changed to make them into a personal prayer, and that will be the form of prayer today.

Part of St Paul's letter to the Christian community in Rome now follows, with a guide afterwards as to the kind of prayer that an individual might decide to express, remembering that *"the Spirit prays within us"*.

All who follow the leading of God's Spirit
    are God's own sons and daughters.
You are not led to be fearful like slaves
    *– instead, God's Spirit **frees** you*
    so that, with a full heart,
    you are enabled to say: "Abba: Father, my Father."
The inner conviction that you have
    of being God's children
    is now endorsed by the Holy Spirit within you.
And so it is clear
    that you are part of God's family circle.
And if you are suffering now,
    remember that you are not only God's children:
    you are his heirs.
Consider how wonderful it is
    that you are entitled
    to inherit the blessings that he has for his people:
    the splendour of the fullness of his life, his glory.

The Spirit helps us in other ways, too.
When we cannot find words as prayer,
    the Spirit himself prays within us
    – prays to the Father (praying for us)
    in a way that could never be put into words!

We know that to all those who love God,
    who are called according to his plan,
    everything that happens works out for good.
Those are the people he chose specially long ago
    to become true images of his Son,
    so that Jesus might be the eldest brother
    of God's large family.

After saying all this, what can we add?
If God is on our side, who can be against us?
As he gave us his Son as a gift,
    surely we can trust God
    to give us the more ordinary things that we need?
We know, too, that Jesus himself now prays for us

in the Father's presence.
And so nothing can ever separate or step in-between
  ourselves and God's great love for us,
  as lived out in Jesus.
No, I am absolutely certain that nothing
  – no trouble or worry,
  no persecution or threats or hardship,
  nor whatever else may come our way
  – can ever part us from God's love
  made visible to us in Jesus Christ our Lord.

(cf. Rom 8¹⁴⁻³⁹)

lowly I read through the scripture passage for a second time...

On my *third* reading I can change the words and extend the phrases to form a personal prayer. Based on the first four lines of that passage, my prayer might start something like this:

Father, I try to follow
  the leading of your Spirit in my life,
  and I rejoice
  that I am your *son/daughter*.
I know that the words *"Do not be afraid"*
  are found many times throughout the Bible,
  and I appreciate that I'm not led
  to be in any way fearful of you
  (as slaves of old might have been
  of those in charge of them).
Instead, you call me to a relationship, Father,
  and your Spirit frees me…

I can continue praying in this way, in speech or in writing.

ACTION

Later today I can look up in the Bible another passage which I can take as personal prayer in similar ways e.g.
  Rom 12⁹⁻¹⁸, 1 Cor 14⁻¹⁸, 2 Cor 4⁵⁻¹⁸, Gal 5¹³⁻²⁶,
  Eph 2⁴⁻¹⁰, Eph 3¹⁴⁻²¹, Phil 4⁴⁻⁹·¹³, Col 3¹²⁻¹⁷, ²³⁻⁴³,
  1 John 4⁷⁻²¹, Rev 21¹⁻⁷

A web-site that offers a short prayer and meditation specific to each day of the year, is by Mark Link, SJ: *'Vision 2000: Praying Scripture in a Contemporary Way': http://v2000.org/index.htm*

'Accepting the embrace of God: Lectio Divina': http://www.ptw.com/ ~ standrab/ld-art.html

Day 46   PRAYING FOR OTHERS

RELAXING

I relax by sitting comfortably and spending a few moments looking in detail at my hands. They may reflect in various ways something of who I am, especially if they bear marks or scars.

(pause)

CALLING TO MIND GOD'S PRESENCE

I ask for God's Spirit to pray in me today…

In odd moments of the day I can call to mind that I am in God's presence. It is a life-giving practice. Some people set an hourly bleeper on their watches as a means to call to mind that they are in God's presence. Such practices can become good habits – in the same way as saying "Thank you" to other people becomes habitual, without needing to think in a determined way about it. I now pause to grow in awareness of God's presence.

(pause)

> Lord,
> **you laid your hands on people
> and brought them new life.
> Lay your hands on me now
> as I start to pray.**

REFLECTING AND PRAYING

Thinking particularly of the poor, I can pray from the psalms:

> "Lord,
> **you are close to the broken-hearted.
> Those whose spirit is crushed
> you will save."**   *Ps 34:19*

We know of the value of praying for others, and occasionally we can make good use of odd moments to bring people to the Lord in prayer. One simple way of doing this (and no-one who is near me need know that I am praying) is to focus on the five fingers of my hand with each serving as a reminder to pray for various groups of people.

I think first of my **THUMB**, being physically nearest to my heart. I pray for **those I love, and those who love me.**

(pause

The **FOREFINGER**. Icons of Jesus often depict him with his forefinger pointing slightly: a sign of him teaching us the Good News. When artists paint individuals as pointing, it is to direct the gaze of the onlooker to someone or something significant (such as in the painting *'Las Meninas'* by Velázquez). Finger-pointing signs in books show the forefinger. A tour guide uses this finger to point the way forward. Thinking of these symbols, I can focus my prayer on all who are involved in 'guiding' others in education. I pray for teachers because *"we can justly say that the future of humanity lies in the hands of those who are strong enough to provide coming generations with reasons for living and hoping".* I pray for **teachers and the young people whom they help to guide.**

(pause

The **MIDDLE FINGER** is the 'tallest'. I pray for **those who have authority, leadership and influence (including the media) in our country, the world, and in the Church.**

(pause

The **FOURTH FINGER** is that which bears a wedding ring. I pray for **those who are married, and for family life**. I pray that society may become more *pro-life* in attitude.

The fourth finger is also the weakest finger, as is attested by those who type or play musical instruments. I pray for **those who are weak and are experiencing difficulties: the ill, dying, bereaved, vulnerable, abused** in our society.

(pause)

The **LITTLE FINGER** is a reminder to pray for **myself**, that I may give first place to God's kingdom (Mt 6^{33}), and may become "less and less, so that Jesus becomes greater" (cf Jn 3^{30}). I pray that I may value and love myself, and so be the better enabled to "love others as I love myself" (cf. Lk 10^{27}). May I be filled with the Holy Spirit and grow as the person God calls me to be.

(pause)

ACTION

Remembering what each finger can represent, I will pray for others again in this way later in the day.

_____

The painting, *'Las Meninas'* (the Maids of Honour) by Velázquez (1599-1660) is accessible on the Internet via *http://www.southern.net/wm/paint/*
The courtier in the background points to the mirror which reflects the image of King Philip IV of Spain.

The quote about *"those who... provide coming generations"* is from the Vatican II document: *'The Church in the Modern World'*, 31 (*'Gaudium et Spes'*).
Documents of the Second Vatican Council: *http://www.christusrex.org/www1/CDHN/v1.html*

See also Day 6)

Day 47   VIEWING THE NIGHT SKY

NEEDED

- *A view at night (or a photograph) of the moon or the stars, or could view shots of the Earth and the Moon from the Apollo 11 landing, via*
  http://nssdc.gsfc.nasa.gov/planetary/lunar/apollo.html

  A NASA Web-Site views shots of the Earth from the Moon:
  http://space.jpl.nasa.gov/

- *The hymn, 'Close to you/I watch the sunrise' or 'O Lord my God...How great thou art', both of which are on the CD/cassette, 'Come Back to Me'.*

RELAXING

I set out to enjoy the view of the Earth, Moon and stars. I relax and become more conscious of my place in the universe, which may lead me to grow in a sense of wonder and awe.

CALLING TO MIND GOD'S PRESENCE

I ask the Holy Spirit to lead me in prayer…

St Ignatius Loyola (1491-1556) could not look at the stars at night without being moved to tears by God's beauty. I spend some moments in silence, reflecting on God's beauty and his presence.

(pause)

God our Father,
　you made the great lights in our sky:
　the sun to rule in the day,
　and the moon and the stars in the night
　– all because your great love
　lasts for ever.
Our sun and moon
　and the stars that you call by name
　all give you praise,
　because they do
　what they were created to do.
Lead me, Father,
　to reflect the light of Christ your Son

and so live fully,
　as, in your love, you created me to do.
Amen.

(cf. Psalms 136⁷⁻⁹, 147⁴, 148³

REFLECTING AND PRAYING

Ralph Waldo Emerson (1803-1882) remarked that:

> *"If the stars were visible only once in a thousand years, we should await the spectacle with breathless interest."*

President Abraham Lincoln (1809-1865) walked in the countryside one night with a friend. He looked up into the sky, named some of the star constellations, and said:

> *"I feel that I am looking into the face of God.*
> *I can see how it might be possible*
> *for someone to look around on earth*
> *and not believe in God,*
> *but I cannot conceive*
> *how anyone could look up into the heavens*
> *and say there is no God."*

A few hours after the Apollo 11 spacecraft had landed on the Moon on 20th July 1969, a capsule was laid in the dust of the moon's surface. It contained Psalm 8, and still remains there. I pray the same psalm:

Lord, our God and King,
　your greatness is seen
　throughout the earth.
When I gaze at the heavens
　which your fingers have formed,
　and look at the moon and the stars
　which you have set there,
　I realise how small we are
　in the magnificence of your creation.
Yet you treasure us
　above all that you have made,
　and you give us control

over all the works of your hands
   – animals both wild and tame,
   birds in the air,
   and the creatures of the sea.
Lord, our God and King,
   your greatness is seen
   throughout the earth.   *(Ps 8)*

can read slowly through the psalm again, reflecting
and praying on each line.

♪ *The hymn could be played.*

ACTION

can start to look at the night sky in a fuller way,
growing in a sense of wonder and awe, as well as of
God's presence.

On Christmas Eve 1968, the opening verses of the Book
of Genesis (1¹-2³: one of the Creation accounts) were
broadcast to Earth by Apollo 8 astronauts as they circled
the Moon. I could access one of the Internet sites looking
back at "the good Earth" set against the blackness of
space. Details of that flight and the Genesis text are
available on:
*http://nssdc.gsfc.nasa.gov/planetary/lunar/
apollo8_xmas.html*

'Welcome to the Planets' (many of the best images
from NASA's planetary exploration):
http://pds.jpl.nasa.gov/planets/
A free e-mail service from NASA is available:
http://science.nasa.gov/news/subscribe.htm

BBC's *'The Sky at Night'*:
http://www.bbc.co.uk/skyatnight/index.shtml
The Planets as seen in the night sky, month by month:
http://www.bbc.co.uk/planets/starmap.shtml
Journey into the heavens:
http://library.advanced.org/28743/
Views of the Solar System:
http://servant.geol.cf.ac.uk/solar/eng/homepage.htm

Day 48   LOOKING BACK OVER THE DAY

RELAXING

As the day draws to a close, I set out to be relaxed, putting into perspective any pressures and problems of the day…

CALLING TO MIND GOD'S PRESENCE

I ask the Holy Spirit to pray in me…

I call to mind that I am in the presence of God…

Lord, the day is far gone
 and the night is at hand.   *Lk 24²⁹*
May the constancy
 of the setting of the sun,
 and its rising
 on those who need it elsewhere,
 remind me
 of your faithfulness and your promise
 to be with us always:
 ready to help us to transform
 darkness into light,
 hatred into love,
 and bitterness into joy. Amen.

REFLECTING AND PRAYING

I can look back over the events of today. I do so not to reminisce or to be in any way hyper-critical of myself, but to reflect and pray – *in God's presence* – asking him to shed light on all that has happened this day, so that I can begin to see things as he might see them…

I can invite Jesus to set off on a journey to re-visit and explore with me the landscape of my day, filled with characters and situations and opportunities. I can start from the feelings I have as the day draws to a close. I ask that I may learn from these experiences as I offer them to the Father through Jesus, my Brother.

I reflect on one or more of the following, focussing particularly on my *attitude*, as that underlies my words and actions:

1 Have I shown respect to all individuals, treating everyone as equals, or have I looked down on or 'excluded' anybody?

2 Have I let someone else's negative attitude dictate the way I chose to respond?

3 Have I brought *'life or death'* to individuals as I have spoken about them or to them? Have I contributed to bringing out the best – or the worst – in others?

4 If acceptance and forgiveness of others are hallmarks of being a Christian, is there anyone tonight whom I don't wish well?

5 Have I been my true self, or have insincerity, pretence and 'masks' been part of my day. If so, why?

ACTION

I will set out tomorrow to be positive and life-giving in my attitude.

A very fine web-site is by the Irish Jesuits – *'Sacred Space'*:
http://www.jesuit.ie/prayer/
Accessing 'Prayer for Today', pressing 'Move On' twice leads to 'Consciousness'. Then, via the 'Prayer Guide', to 'Review of Consciousness'.

Another 'Examen of Consciousness' is:
http://www.jesuit.org/pilgrim/examen.html

The Practice of Awareness Meditation:
http://www2.bc.edu/ ~ anderso/sr/pam.html

'Daily Ways to Pray' (through the Spiritual Exercises of St Ignatius Loyola):
http://www.nwjesuits.org/dailyw/index.htm

Day 49   A BUSY DAY TOMORROW

NEEDED

- *To be in a place of privacy and quiet.*
- *The hymn, 'Abide with me', on the CD/cassette, 'Holy One of Israel'.*

RELAXING

In a comfortable position, I focus on relaxing the muscles in various parts of my body in turn…

I pray the words of a verse of the hymn, *'Dear Lord and Father of Mankind'*:

Drop thy still dews of quietness,
Till all our strivings cease.
Take from our souls the strain and stress,
And let our ordered lives confess
The beauty of thy peace,
The beauty of thy peace.

(pause)

CALLING TO MIND GOD'S PRESENCE

I ask the Holy Spirit who lives within me, to pray in me…

With my elbows touching my side, and my arms held out in front, and my palms upturned (a sign of openness to God) I can repeat several times the following words, whilst keeping my eyes closed (or looking at an image that represents Jesus):

Lord, I come into your presence
with an open heart.

♪ *The hymn, 'Abide with me', could be played.*

REFLECTING AND PRAYING

I can reflect on the implications of the following words of Goethe, the German philosopher (1749-1832):

> *"Tell me what you are busy about,*
> *and I will tell you what you are."*

(pause)

Martin Luther, the Church reformer, said:

> *"Tomorrow I plan to work, work,*
> *from early until late.*
> *In fact, I have so much to do*
> *that I shall spend the first three hours*
> *in prayer."*

Whilst many of us have genuine commitments that prevent us from doing as Luther urges of himself, the message about the priority of prayer is clear.

The great leader of India, Mahatma Gandhi (1869-1948), wrote:

> *I am neither a man of letters*
> *nor of Science,*
> *but I humbly claim to be a man of prayer.*
> *It is prayer that has saved my life.*
> *Without prayer*
> *I would have lost my reason*
> *a long time ago.*
> *I did not lose my peace of soul*
> *– in spite of many trials –*
> *because the peace came to me*
> *through prayer.*
> *One can live several days without food,*
> *but not without prayer.*
> *Prayer is the key to each morning,*
> *and the lock to every evening.*
> *This is my teaching:*
> *let everyone try this experience*
> *and they will find that daily prayer*
> *will add something new to their lives.*

God our Father,
   amidst the busy-ness and noise
   of daily life,
   I ask you to bring it home to me
   how much I need
   time and quiet for myself,
   in which I can become
   more attuned with myself
   and more at one with you, my God.
As I am then able
   to grow more in your image and likeness
   and be re-created,
   inspire me to be creative
   and develop to the full
   the talents you have given me
   for the benefit of those people
   you place into my life. Amen.

ACTION

During the course of tomorrow I can make use of this
prayer of Lord Astley (1579-1652), spoken before the
Battle of Edgehill during the English Civil War:
   O Lord,
   you know how busy I must be this day.
   If I forget you, do not forget me."

Details about the hymn, *'Abide with me'*, may be found
on the Internet at *'The Cyber Hymnal'* (along with the
tune):
http://tch.simplenet.com/index.htm#titles
Fuller details about the hymn are available in the
author's 3-volume book, *'Praying Each Day of the Year'* –
see *'Further Resources'* at the back of this book.

"A man of letters" in the Gandhi quote, refers to the
letters that someone might have after their name,
generally denoting educational, professional or
honorific titles e.g. BA, MBE.

"ENFOLDED IN THE GENTLENESS OF GOD"

(Julian of Norwich

NEEDED

- *Some gentle relaxing music.*
- *The song, 'Only a Shadow', from the CD/cassette, 'Come Back to Me'.*

RELAXING

As I play the relaxing music, I place myself in a comfortable position, close my eyes, and focus on and relax parts of my body in turn…

I can then reflect on these words:
"We are all enfolded
in the gentleness of God."   (Julian of Norwich)

I turn off the music

CALLING TO MIND GOD'S PRESENCE

There is the story of the young man
whose wife dies suddenly from illness.
Their 6-year-old daughter
was as heart-broken as her father.
One night she woke up
and could hear her father
sobbing in his bedroom.

The next day she made a present
and wrapped it up,
and gave it to her father.
He took off the coloured paper
and opened the small box,
only to look at his daughter
in puzzlement.

"It's empty, Elizabeth," he said.
"No it's not, Daddy," she replied.
"I heard you crying last night,
and so I've blown kisses into it.
They're my present to you."

That night the young man sobbed again
but, this time,
he was cherishing the love of his daughter.
From then on,
he kept the treasure of her box
in a special place in his room.

I pause to think of God's love for me: God who is present with me now…

♪ *I could play the song, 'Only a shadow'.*

REFLECTING AND PRAYING

My prayer – however brief – at the end of a day, may focus in five 'areas':
- presence
- rejoicing
- thanks
- sorrow
- asking

The second element – rejoicing – should always be included, especially as it reminds me to focus in my life on what is positive. I am glad about certain good things of the day. 'Rejoicing' leads into 'thanksgiving'.

These five elements in prayer I may express simply, perhaps starting in the following way, pausing for a moment after each:

- **Lord, it's good to be here**
  in your presence…

- **I rejoice that…, I'm glad about…**

- **I give thanks for all your blessings**
  and for all that has been good this day,
  especially…

- **I'm sorry for…**

- **I ask you…**

My prayer of "asking" might include requesting that I (and those I love and who love me) may rest in peace this night, surrounded by God's love and blessings.

I offer to God my imagination, my subconscious and my unconscious, especially as they help put me in touch with hidden inner realities of my personality and experience. And so, having prayer as the last thoughts of my waking day, may help to 'free' God to work in other ways 'within me' during the night. Just before going to sleep I can repeat slowly a few times:

> *"Into your hands, Lord,*
> *I commend my spirit"*   *Ps 316; Lk 2346*

committing myself into the hands of our Father, as Jesus did on the cross.

ACTION

Those who choose to take up this practice of prayer focussing on five 'areas' at the end of the day may, at first, be helped by a mnemonic to recall the first letters of **p**resence, **r**ejoicing, **t**hanks, **s**orrow, **a**sking – e.g. *'**P**lease **R**eturn **T**o **S**ender's **A**ddress'*.

A web-site specific to each day of the year is found at: *http://www.americancatholic.org/* and then select *'Minute Meditations'*.

The sacraments – being special occasions of experiencing God – have been described as "God's kisses".

A postscript
"To make an end is to make a beginning" (T.S.Eliot)

The two disillusioned disciples on their journey to Emmaus were convinced that it was 'the end of the road' for them. Dramatically their lives changed forever as they recognised the risen Jesus in their midst, walking with them. My journey, too, can be one of great discovery as I come face-to-face with God who walks with me on holy ground (Gen 3^8, Ex 3^6, Lk 24$^{13\text{-}35}$).

Have I encountered and recognised God in recent weeks? Have I been growing closer to him? Am I becoming more aware of God's presence in my life? Am I gaining a deeper lived experience of God's personal love? Am I growing in understanding and love of myself as well as of others, appreciating that each is a temple of God 1 Cor 3^{16})? Do I feel that God's love and power have enabled me to do what otherwise I might not have done? Am I experiencing some inner peace, even though difficult circumstances of life may not have changed? Am I more likely to forgive – and know that I am forgiven – not so much by determined effort, but in the confidence that God himself never stops loving? Am I better able to identify with and 'feel' for others? Am I seeing a greater unity in life? Am I valuing silence more? Am I growing in my understanding of God's providence? Am I more convinced that the "path on which I approach God leads through the very middle of my ordinary daily life" (K.Rahner)? Each of these, surely, indicates that the Spirit has been at work and my heart has been touched as I have set out to pray.

At the end of *The Wizard of Oz*, Dorothy talks of the adventures she has had on her journey: *"I've been to many strange and marvellous places, looking for something that was right here all along…right in my own back yard."* A similar profound message lies in T S Eliot's *'Little Gidding'* (from *'The Four Quartets'*):

> *"We shall not cease from exploration,*
> *And the end of all our exploring*
> *Will be to arrive where we started*
> *And know the place for the first time.*
> *To make an end is to make a beginning.*
> *The end is where we start from."*

It is likely that there will be much in this book that is still 'untapped', and it would be helpful to proceed through the course again, either now or at a later date, as well as 'dipping' into certain 'Days'. Beyond this page is a section entitled *'Other Resources'*, which names some books, cassettes, CD-Roms, and additional Internet information. Some of these – and most particularly the Bible itself – can be of further help in the personal journey of faith and discovery. Of the many excellent web-sites named in the book, several give prayers and reflections specific to the day, each forming their own "course" in prayer.

Important and useful as other resources are, they would, however, be a hindrance if they were used to explore *about* prayer to the extent of neglecting *to pray*. In that context, I might arrive at a similar conclusion to that which Hilaire Belloc invited his readers to draw from the final words of his book on sailing: *'Dear reader, read less and sail more'.*

"THE STILL SMALL VOICE OF CALM"

('Dear Lord and Father of Mankind'

This reflection returns us to our 'beginning' again with the Old Testament, full of promises of renewal as well as reminders that the Lord chooses to be with us and calls us his very own. To make an end is, indeed, to make a beginning (cf T.S. Eliot).

There in the wilderness
    the angel of the Lord touched Elijah and said:
    "Get up and eat well, or the journey will be too much for you."
Elijah looked around,
    and there beside him he found bread baked on hot stones
    and a jar of water.
Strengthened by that food
    he walked for forty days and forty nights
    until he reached Mount Horeb.
This was Sinai,
    the mountain where Moses had seen the burning bush
    and encountered God:
    the place of the Ten Commandments
    and God's Covenant with his people.

There, on Mount Horeb,
    Elijah went into a cave
    and spent the night.
In the morning
    he was told to go out
    and stand on the mountain
    because the Lord was about to pass by.

There came a mighty wind,
    so strong that it caused landslides
    and split rocks apart
    – but the Lord was not in the wind.

After the wind there came an earthquake
    - but the Lord was not in the earthquake.

After the earthquake there came a fire
    – but the Lord was not in the fire.

And then after the fire
    there came a gentle, whispering breeze.
And in that silence
    the Lord spoke to Elijah.

(cf 1 Kings 19:5-16)

FURTHER RESOURCES

BOOKS

'Praying Each Day of the Year' by Nicholas Hutchinson, FSC. This three-volume book offers a reflection and a prayer specific to each day of the year e.g. referring to the birth or death of an historical figure, or the anniversary of an event or discovery. A very useful tool for praying alone, or for use by teachers and others leading collective acts of worship. Volume 1 includes an invaluable index to locate 600 key passages throughout the Bible. Excerpts from the books are read each week on BBC Radio. Sample pages (as also for *'Walk In My Presence'*) may be obtained from the author (see the Introduction for the address) on receipt of a stamped addressed envelope. Published by Matthew James, Chelmsford:
January-April: ISBN 1-898366-30-6   (176 pages)
May-August: ISBN 1-898366-31-4   (200 pages)
September-December: ISBN 1-898366-31-4   (208 pages)

'Walk In My Presence' by Nicholas Hutchinson, FSC. Whilst there are books available of prayers and of anthologies of readings, there are very few of prayer services. *'Walk In My Presence'* answers that need, with prayers and readings that are themed and integrated from many Catholic, Protestant and Orthodox sources. Some 40 prayer services focus, for example, on God's presence, creation, the Incarnation, justice and peace, the vision of Jesus, morning and night prayer, forgiveness, sickness, growing older. Published by Matthew James, Chelmsford in May 2000: ISBN 1-898366-608.

'Come Lord Jesus' by Lucien Deiss: World Library Publications, Chicago (1981): ISBN 0-937690-18-X. This book helps to 'open up' the treasure of the Scriptures. Inspiring prayers that are biblically-based. A fine resource. (326 pages).

'The Cry of the Deer' by David Adam (156 pages), sub-titled, *'Meditations on the Hymn of St Patrick'*: Triangle/SPCK Press (1987), ISBN 0-281-04284-5. This is a book to take if about to be marooned on a desert island! It offers much richness to be 'tapped' for prayer and reflection. David Adam has several other books on Celtic Spirituality e.g. *'The Edge of Glory: Prayers in the Celtic Tradition'* and *'The Eye of the Eagle: Meditations on the hymn, "Be Thou My Vision"'.*

'YOU' by Mark Link, SJ – Argus Communications (1976), ISBN 0-913592-78-1. The book is sub-titled: 'Prayer for Beginners and Those Who Have Forgotten How'. (156 pages).

'A Child's Book of Prayer in Art' (32 pages) by Sister Wendy Beckett: Dorling Kindersley (1995). ISBN: 0-7513-5276-4. Sister Wendy offers inspiration not only to children but to those who try to follow the Gospel injunction to become like little children! The book is an 'eye-opener', leading the reader to discover with the author that *"Looking at art is one way of listening to God."* Most touching insights are shared in her comprehensive *'Sister Wendy's Story of Painting'* (400 pages), also by Dorling Kindersley (1994): ISBN 0-7513-0133-7.

'The Return of the Prodigal Son' by Henri Nouwen. DLT: 152 pages, ISBN 0-232-52078-X. A wonderful book which explores implications from Jesus' parable, as depicted in Rembrandt's painting of the same name (see 'Day 10'). The author leads the reader to see self in the lost son, in the elder son, and in the Father. Another 'desert-island' book!

'God of Surprises' by Gerard Hughes, SJ. Published by DLT in 1985 (ISBN: 0-232-51664-2). Undoubtedly one of the great books of spiritual guidance. Highly recommended to anyone who is serious about encountering God for themselves. (162 pages).

'Pause for Thought with Frank Topping' (240 pages) by Frank Topping (1981): Lutterworth Press, Guildford: ISBN 0-7188-2524-1. Touching prayers with which we can readily identify are based on the ordinariness of daily life.

'Gathering the Fragments' by Edward Farrell, Ave Maria Press, 1987: ISBN 0-87793-361-8. Another inspiring book to pack if about to be marooned! (102 pages).

'Loving Lord'. Denis Blackledge, SJ has written several handy booklets of inspiring prayers, sub-titled *'Seasons'*, *'Moments'*, *'Horizons'*, *'Tidelines'*, and *'Encounters'* (1991-1995): each about 64 pages. Published by Sanctuary Books, 1 Winckley Square, Preston PR1 3JJ. Denis broadcasts these and other prayers (such as from *'Praying Each Day of the Year'*) on BBC Radio Lancashire.

'Clouds and Glory' (0-281-05034-1) and *'Traces of Glory'* (0-281-05199-2) are very fine books of intercessory prayers by David Adam (SPCK): prayers that focus on the readings for each Sunday of the Anglican liturgy. Inspiring prayers.

'Prayers of Intercession, Book 1' (0-86209-964-1) and *'Prayers of Intercession, Book 2'* (0-86209-978-1). These books by Susan Sayers (published by Kevin Mayhew) are of imaginatively written intercessory prayers which could be used by individuals or by groups in public worship (e.g. in the Eucharist or in the 'Prayer of the Church' or with youth/school groups).

'Come and Pray' by Donal Neary, SJ (72 pages). The Columba Press (1988), ISBN 0-948183-53-5. His prayers are based on Gospel characters. He has written several other short books of prayers and reflections.

'Sadhana: A Way to God – Christian Exercises in Eastern Form' by Anthony de Mello, SJ (140 pages): Doubleday Image, 1984. ISBN 0-385-19614-8. Along with another book of his, *'Wellsprings'*, Eastern insights are offered in his challenging Christian meditations.

'As Bread That Is Broken' by Peter van Breemen (192 pages), Dimension Books, 1974. ISBN 087-1930528. A classic book of spirituality reflecting the fullness of God's love for each individual (pg 44).

'Daysprings' by Margaret Silf, (DLT, 1999, 276 pages). ISBN 0-232-52350-9. Gives a brief reflection – but very much to the point – on one of the Scripture passages for each weekday and Sunday in the RC 2/3 Year Cycle. A very fine starting point for reflection and prayer.

'Prayer for Pilgrims' by Sheila Cassidy, Fount, Collins, 1980 (192 pages) ISBN 0-00-6254-19-5. Helpful reflections on praying in daily life.

'The William Barclay Prayer Book', edited by Ronald Barclay, published by Fount in 1994: ISBN 0-00-627862-0. As well as prayers for special occasions or amidst difficulties, the book includes 70 days of reflective prayers and scriptural readings. (298 pages).

'Praying Our Experiences' by Joseph Schmidt, FSC (St Mary's Press, Winona, 1980). ISBN 088489-1135 (57 pages). *'I believe that praying one's experiences is exceedingly common among people who, ironically, not understanding it to be prayer, condemn themselves for not praying'* (pg 6).

'The Spiritual Exercise Book' by Una Kroll, Macmillan Books (ISBN 028399455). Explores ways of praying using imagery, posture and physical movement.

'Six Ways to Pray from Six Great Saints' by Gloria Hutchinson, St Anthony Messenger Press (1982), ISBN 0-86716-007-1 (152 pages). Explores ways of praying of Francis and Clare of Assisi, Ignatius, Thérèse of Lisieux, Teresa of Avila, and John of the Cross.

'The Classics of Catholic Spirituality' by Peter Cameron, OP (144 pages), published by the Society of St Paul, New York, 1996. Individual chapters explore (with quotations) in a very readable way the spirituality of Augustine, Francis, Julian of Norwich, Catherine of Siena, Thomas à Kempis, Ignatius Loyola, John of the Cross, Teresa of Avila, Brother Lawrence and Thérèse of Lisieux. ISBN: 0-8189-0743-6.

SCRIPTURAL BOOKS

'The Psalms – the Grail Psalms (An Inclusive Language Version)' – beautifully written and an accurate translation (directly from the Hebrew) of the psalms, retaining their poetic rhythm and inspiration. (216 pages) ISBN 0-00-599994-4. The text is also available on the Internet (see 'Day 38').

'A Shorter Morning and Evening Prayer' – being one of the versions of *'The Prayer of the Church: The Psalter of the Divine Office'* (as mentioned in 'Day 8'), Collins: ISBN 0-00-599734-8, 492 pages.

An excellent, prayerful and very readable commentary on 'The Prayer of the Church' is *'The School of Prayer (An Introduction to the Divine Office for all Christians)'* by New Zealander, John Brook (441 pages). Published by HarperCollins in 1992. ISBN 0-00-599216-8.

'The New Lion Encyclopaedia of the Bible' (320 pages) is not only superbly presented and illustrated (including classical paintings), but gives a most excellent overview of each book of the Bible, as well as general background. The book goes far beyond being an encyclopaedia because it offers significant help in 'opening up the Scriptures'. Lion Publishers: ISBN 0-7459-3922-8

'The Bible from Scratch' by Simon Jenkins (156 pages): Lion, ISBN 0-7459-1004-1. The book offers in line-drawing format a short but comprehensive overview of each book of the Bible.

Praying St Mark's Gospel by Gerald O'Mahoney, SJ (136 pages; 1990) Geoffrey Chapman: ISBN: 0-225-66610-3. As the title suggests, a very prayerful approach, 'placing self' into the Gospel.

CD-ROMS

'The Jerusalem Bible (1966 Edition)', Churchill Systems, Tadcaster. Along with the full text of each book of the Bible there are maps and time charts and notes. Especially useful is the 'search' facility' which, at the touch of a button, displays in whichever book(s) of the Bible you have indicated, all the texts that include, for example, the word "light". A great 'enabling tool'.

'Religious Clip Art' by Steve Erspamer. ISBN 1-898366-18-7, published as three books by Liturgy Training Publications (Chicago), the same material is available on CD-Rom by Matthew James Publishing, Chelmsford. Nearly 1500 monochrome images focus on the 3-year cycle of the RC Liturgy of Sundays and Feastdays. The mediaeval/manuscript-type of clip art is most inspirational, offering 'picture-images' that, when used with the appropriate biblical texts (which are listed), cannot but lead to prayer. Extremely useful is the search-facility – e.g. for 'sheep' or 'candle' – readily bringing those images to the screen. The most highly-recommended of all religious clip-art – not only for use in newsletters etc., but as a means in personal prayer. The graphics in the present book are also by Steve Erspamer.

CASSETTES of talks on prayer
Talks on prayer by. Dr Sheila Cassidy, Dr Donald English, Fr Gerard Hughes, Cardinal Basil Hume, and Mrs Grace Sheppard are available from the Centre for Spirituality, Westminster Cathedral, 42 Francis St., London SW1P 1QW (Tel: 0171-798-9055). See the Internet web-site for 'The Centre of Spirituality', via: *http://www.westminstercathedral.org.uk/*

CDs/CASSETTES of music
Links are made throughout this book to songs on three discs of Marilla Ness:
'Come Back to Me', *'He Touched Me'*, and *'Holy One of Israel'*. *'The Marilla Ness Songbook'* (ISBN 0-9523808-0-3), published by 'Merciful Love Music', 1994 (78 pages), includes the words and music for all the hymns mentioned in *'Lord, Teach us to Pray'*.

'I will not forget you' and *'Abba, Father'* are the two most popular of Carey Landry singing his own songs.

'Laudate: Music of Taizé' (produced in Dublin) is probably the most popular album of Taizé music. The St Thomas More Centre in London have produced two cassettes of Taizé music: *'Watch and Pray'*, and *'I am With You Always'*.

The St Thomas More Centre (in conjunction with OCP Publications in the USA) have two cassettes of some of their more well-used music: *'St Thomas More Group's Greatest Hits'* – *Volumes 1 and 2*.

MORE INTERNET RESOURCES
These are in addition to those detailed throughout the book.

PRAYER/SPIRITUALITY

Numerous very fine prayer sites (including re illness, seasons of the Church's Year, the Lord's Prayer) can be accessed via:
http://www.cptryon.org/

Lent: A Call to Conversion:
http://www.americancatholic.org/welcome/special_pages/lent/lent_home.html

A Lent Site:
http://www.udayton.edu/~ campmin/lent.html

'Daily Reflections' accessed via Liguori Publications:
http://www.liguori.org/

Keeping a Prayer Journal:
http://web.wt.net/ ~ wayne/prayjrn.html and *http://www.mjp-books.com/religion.htm*

Prayer Journal:
http://www.wtp.net/ ~ anchor/follow3.html

'The Text This Week' from the Revised Common Lectionary, and worship hints and resources, including specific web-sites of religious art particular to the feastday:
http://www.textweek.com/

Oremus – Anglican daily prayer (including the music of hymns):
http://www.oremus.org/

Celebrating Common Prayer (an Anglican version of the Daily Office):
http://justus.anglican.org/ ~ ss/ccp/

Bible Browser (a search engine to locate a word or phrase in the Bible):
http://mama.stg.brown.edu/webs/bible_browser/pbform.shtml

Prayer for Each Day (several short prayers for each day):
http://www.bobjanet.demon.co.uk/prytoday.html

Spirituality for Today:
http://www.spirituality.org/index.html

Scripts of recent Radio 4 'Thought for the Day' Broadcasts by Lavinia Byrne IBVM:
http://easyweb.easynet.co.uk/ ~ cybernun/Broadcas.htm#BroadcastScripts

Assisi and St Francis:
http://www.assind.perugia.it/umbria/assisi/assing.htm

The lives and writings of Mediaeval English Mystics:
http://www.anamchara.com/mystics/

Julian of Norwich:
http://www.luminarium.org/medlit/julian.htm

Julian of Norwich: *'Revelations of Divine Love'*:
http://ccel.wheaton.edu/julian/revelations/

Dominic's Nine Ways of Prayer:
http://www.op.org/domcentral/places/stjude/NineWays.html

John Henry Newman:
http://ic.net/ ~ erasmus/RAZ22.HTM

English Literature and Religion:
http://www.inform.umd.edu/ENGL/englfac/WPeterson/ELR/elr.htm

Dietrich Bonhoeffer:
http://www.cyberword.com/bonhoef/

The Tablet, weekly religious periodical (including many links):
http://www.thetablet.co.uk

Centering Prayer:
http://www.centeringprayer.org/
and
http://209.1.224.12/Athens/Delphi/5655/essay/essay.html

Spiritual and Mystical Texts:
http://www.ucc.uconn.edu/~ das93006/spirit.html

Sanctuary (Celtic Spirituality)
http://www.angelfire.com/in/sanctuary/

Celtic Spirituality:
http://english.glendale.cc.ca.us/christ.html

Some prayers of Celtic spirituality
http://www.smo.uhi.ac.uk/gaidhlig/corpus/Carmina/

Celtic and Old English Saints
http://www.nireland.com/orthodox/saints.htm

Iona Spirituality Institute:
http://www.iona.edu/stu_life/ministry/ISI.htm

The Biblelands Project – a tour of and reflections on people and places of the bible, including many photographs:
http://www.mustardseed.net

Photographs of Palestine:
http://cweb.middlebury.edu/cr/powell/index.htm

Palestine in the Time of Jesus – resources:
http://www.stolaf.edu/people/kchanson/ptj.html

Holy Land Online:
http://www.holy-land-online.com/

Model of Jerusalem in the time of Jesus:
http://www.holy-land-online.com/temple/model.htm

From Jesus to Christ: the first Christians: a wide-ranging site including an overview of each Gospel:
http://www.pbs.org/wgbh/pages/frontline/shows/religion/

The playing of (and details about) hymns:
http://www.littleflower.org/slf/music.htm
and also:
http://tch.simplenet.com/index.htm#titles

Virtual Religion Index (accessing all World Religions):
http://religion.rutgers.edu/links/vrindex.html

CHURCHES/DIOCESES/THEOLOGY etc

A site giving access to many Churches – RC, Orthodox, Anglican, Baptist, Lutheran, Reformed and Presbyterian:
http://www.blackwellpublishers.co.uk/religion/

The Anglican Church *(including morning and evening prayer):*
http://www.cofe.anglican.org/services/index.html

The Westminster Abbey site includes
"20th Century Martyrs: 10 new statues", giving details of each martyr. The site also gives access to many Anglican and other dioceses:
http://www.westminster-abbey.org/

Many Anglican and other Church links:
http://www.andrew.ang-md.org/anglicanlinks.html

The Catholic Church in England and Wales:
http://www.tasc.ac.uk/cc/index.htm

Catholic Church in Scotland:
http://www.catholic-scotland.org.uk/

Westminster Cathedral *(including re prayer and spirituality):*
http://www.westminstercathedral.org.uk/

The Vatican/The Holy See *(including museums):*
http://www.vatican.va/

A very extensive and wide-ranging RC site, with links beyond counting:
http://www.catolicos.org/

Catholic Resources on the Net:
http://www.cs.cmu.edu/People/spok/catholic.html

Catholic Information Network:
http://www.cin.org

'Catechism of the Catholic Church' *(with Search Engine):*
http://www.christusrex.org/www1/CDHN/ccc.html
or, if difficult to access, can do so via:
http://www.christusrex.org/
being a wide-ranging web-site

Theology Library:
http://www.mcgill.pvt.k12.al.us/jerryd/cathmob.htm

Religious Education Centre:
http://www.theresite.org.uk

R.E. Net:
http://www.cant.ac.uk/renet/

'On-Line Books' (i.e. whole texts) that can be downloaded from the Internet) for no charge:
http://www.cs.cmu.edu/books.html
Then choose "Subjects" and "Christianity" for a very wide range of available texts.

The Christian Catacombs of Rome:
http://www.catacombe.roma.it/

Symbols in Christian Art and Architecture:
http://www.fastlane.net/homepages/wegast/symbols/symbols.htm

National Retreat Association (Retreat Houses):
http://www.retreats.org.uk/

De La Salle Brothers:
http://www.lasalle.org/ and *http://www.dlsnet.demon.co.uk/index.htm*

Religious Orders:
http://www.geocities.com/~ catolicos/comunidadesreligiosas.htm

Christmas Customs *(focus on any of the named countries to discover various Christmas customs):*
http://christmas.com/worldview/

Electronic Greetings Cards by the Franciscans and the Poor Clare Sisters:
http://www.franciscancards.com/

The Enneagram:
http://www.enneagraminstitute.com/

Reuters 'World Environment News' is available regularly as an e-mail (free of charge) from:
http://www.planetark.org

Hyperhistory Online (including time-lines of world history):
http://www.hyperhistory.com/online_n2/History_n2/a.html

BBC Web Guide (an overview that gives access to the BBC's very extensive web-site:
http://www.bbc.co.uk/webguide/

Dogpile: an extremely effective Search Engine (incorporating several search engines):
http://www.dogpile.com/

ART

The Web Gallery of Art:
http://gallery.euroweb.hu/index.html

WebMuseum, Paris:
http://www.southern.net/wm/paint/

Virtual Art Museum (CGFA):
http://sunsite.auc.dk/cgfa/

Artcyclopedia:
http://artcyclopedia.com/index.html

Image Gallery Fine Arts:
http://www.christusrex.org/www2/art/

A resource of Art of the Annunciation, Nativity and Epiphany:
http://www.execpc.com/ ~ tmuth/st_john/xmas/art.htm

'The Passion and Resurrection of Christ in Art':
http://www.execpc.com/ ~ tmuth/easter/art.htm

'Meditation with Art':
http://landru.i-link-2.net/shnyves/Art_in_Meditation.html

The Book of Kells:
http://www.osl.state.or.us/csimages/kells/bk.htm

Churches, Cathedrals and Art:
http://www.christusrex.org/www1/splendors/splendors.html

Celtic web art:
http://hometown.aol.com/Cyrion7/celtic/index.htm

ICONS

Orthodox Byzantine Icons:
http://www.skete.com/

Heavenly Visions Byzantine Icon Studio:
http://www.heavenlyvisions.com/

Icons and Iconography:
http://ourworld.compuserve.com/homepages/seraphim_rose_books/icons.htm

Some Orthodox icons:
http://www.ocf.org/OrthodoxPage/icons/icons.html

More Orthodox icons:
http://www.mcauley.acu.edu.au/ ~ yuri/Icons/icons.htm

Orthodox Icons Today:
http://icons.virtualave.net/

Some modern icons:
http://maple.lemoyne.edu/ ~ bucko/andre.html
and a modern icon of Jesus, having been taken down from the cross, being held by his mother:
http://maple.lemoyne.edu/ ~ bucko/krivak.html

Icons by Christopher Gosey:
http://www.artmax.com/artmax/docs/gosey.htm

Acknowledgements

The publishers are grateful for receiving permission to include the following extracts:

Day 1 from *Encountering Light,* © 1975, Gonville ffrench-Beytagh, published by Harper Collins Ltd, London.

Day 5 from *Laboratories of the Spirit,* by R.S. Thomas, © 1973, Rupert Hart Davies Ltd, London.

Day 6 & Day 19 from *The Jerusalem Bible,* published and copyright 1966, 1967 and 1968, by Darton Longman and Todd Ltd and Doubleday and Co Inc.

Day 11 from *Poustinia: Christian Spirituality of the East for Western Man,* © 1975, Catherine de Hueck Doherty, published by Ave Maria Press, P.O.Box 428, Notre Dame, Indiana 46556-0428, USA.

Day 12 & Day 44 from *To be a Pilgrim,* © 1984, Cardinal Basil Hume OSB, published by St Paul Publications, Middlegreen, Slough SL3 6BT.

Day 16 from *True Wilderness,* © 1983, H.A.Williams, published by Harper Collins Ltd, London.

Day 25 from *A Bible Prayer Book for Today,* © 1976, Peter de Rosa, published by Harper Collins Ltd, London.

Day 26 from *Loving Lord: Encounters,* & Day 31 from *Loving Lord: Seasons,* © 1995,1991, Denis Blackledge, SJ, Priests' House, Sacred Heart Church, 17 Talbot Road, Blackpool FY1 1LB.

Day 32 from *Mister God, this is Anna,* © 1977 Fynn, published by Harper Collins Ltd, London.

Day 32 from *The Broken Body,* © 1988, Jean Vanier, Published by Darton Longman & Todd Ltd.

Day 37 from *Celtic Meditations,* © 1976, Edward J Farrell, published Dimension Books, PO Box 811, Denville, New Jersey 07834, USA.

Day 39 from *The Gospel of John - Volume 1,* © 1965,William Barclay, published by St Andrew Press, Edinburgh.

Day 41 from *God of Surprises,* © 1985, Gerard Hughes SJ, published by Darton Longman & Todd Ltd.

Postscript extract from *Little Gidding* from *The Four Quartets* in the *Complete Poems and Plays of TS Eliot*, © 1969 Valerie Eliot, published by Faber and Faber.

INDEX

Numbers refer to the 'Day' rather than to the page.
The main scriptural texts are mentioned in this Index.